CATHOLIC BAPTISMS IN WESTERN PENNSYLVANIA, 1799 - 1828

Father Peter Helbron's
Greensburg Register

CATHOLIC BAPTISMS IN WESTERN PENNSYLVANIA, 1799 - 1828

Father Peter Helbron's Greensburg Register

Reprinted from Records of the
American Catholic Historical Society of Philadelphia

With an Added Index of Names

Baltimore
GENEALOGICAL PUBLISHING CO., INC.
1985

Originally published in installments in
*Records of the American Catholic Historical
Society of Philadelphia* between September 1915
and December 1917.
Reprinted, with an added index, by
Genealogical Publishing Co., Inc.
Baltimore, Maryland 1985.
Index copyright © 1985 by Genealogical
Publishing Co., Inc. All Rights Reserved.
Library of Congress Catalogue Card Number 84-73331
International Standard Book Number 0-8063-1113-4
Made in the United States of America

FATHER PETER HELBRON'S BAPTISMAL REGISTER AT SPORTSMAN'S HALL, PENNA.

BY P. FELIX FELLMER, O. S. B.

THE Church Registers[1] of Fr. Peter Helbron, O. M. Cap., are the best proofs of his extensive missionary journeys in Western Pennsylvania during the first decade of the nineteenth century. At least seven counties were visited by him until he received colaborers in this vineyard of the Lord. These counties formed a semicircle with the western slopes of the Allegheny mountains as a diameter, viz. Westmoreland, Fayette, Washington, Greene, Allegheny, Butler, and Armstrong. How much farther north he extended his trips can only be surmised from an expression in one of his letters to Bishop Carrol, "As far as the lake," and from a tradition that he went as far as Lake Erie,

Within this area he established stations or built mission churches, four of which owed their foundation to his zeal or at least to his earnest coöperation. With the baptismal register as our guide, two of these communities, situated north of the Allegheny River, must draw our particular attention both on account of the number

[1] The first Register of Sportsmanshall, now St. Vincent Archabbey, is a small folio of 154 pages, bound in half morocco and contains the baptism, marriage and burial records of Fathers Peter Helbron, Charles B. Maguire, Terrence McGirr, and of visiting priests Prince-priest Gallitzin, F. H. O'Brien, etc. On the first page Father Helbron in his methodical way has a summary of his baptisms from 1799-1808 (the year when F. O'Brien arrived) viz : 578, and on one of the last pages he records the paschal confessions from 1801-1815, viz : 2176. The marriage and burial records are incomplete.

5

of baptisms as well as on account of their special mention. These were Slippery Rock and Buffalo. [Boflo, Buofflo, Bufloo]. Thus in October, 1803, Father Helbron baptized eighteen persons at Slippery Rock and during the same month thirty-nine in Bofflo; in September and October, 1805, his baptismal register contains eighty-four baptisms from this same district; [In a letter of the same year he even speaks of ninety]; and during the month of October, 1812, he entered fifteen on the same day and from the same place. These missionary visits were, however, not the only ones during these years, as other entries testify, and the same baptismal register proves that sometimes the faithful from those localities brought their children a distance of forty miles for baptism.[1] This happened especially from 1800-1806 when F. Helbron was the only resident priest in this locality. His visit to Buffalo in 1812 seems to have been occasioned by a vacancy in the pastorship in that place.

Taking again the baptismal register as our criterion, F. Helbron must have divided his missionary field into two districts, the northern and southern, and the journey from Sportsmanshall to Buffalo seems to have taken him three days.[2] Likewise the Baptismal Register proves that he made his first entries on separate leaves and after his return copied these notes into the parish records. Otherwise repetitions of the same names in the same records would be impossible. We can imagine our missionary, whilst attending to this "office work," being called away by other duties and after his return retran-

---

[1] RECORD, Sept. 1915; p. 258; September 6, 1801; p. 259, February 21, 1802; p. 261, June 6, 1802.

[2] September 22, 1805 (Sunday), Fr. Helbron records a baptism in Sportsmanshall which seems to be evident both from the name of the family of the child as well as from those of the sponsors. September 26 (Thursday), he records his first baptism in Buffalo (Bofflo).

scribing some entries by mistake.[1] At first sight the number of baptisms at Bofflo may seem excessive, especially during October of 1805. But upon close investigation the large number (84) will not appear so extraordinary. His entries prove that on this missionary journey he baptized repeatedly several members of one and the same family, but after his return he rarely registered them in succession. These families were probably immigrants who had lived years without having seen a priest. In this manner nineteen baptisms are divided among only six families, viz., six children of John and Petronilla (once Eleanora) Diamond; four children of Henry and Ann McLaughlin; three children of Patrick and Mary McBride, etc. Moreover in 1803 Father Helbron entered the baptisms of the two places, Slippery Rock and Bofflo, separately; in the second visit, in 1805, however, he registered them indiscriminately. There cannot be any doubt that he was at Slippery Rock also on that occasion. The same family names occur then as in 1803, viz. John and Cecilia Roger, John and Margaret Schmidt, Anthony and Bridget Schorty, etc., and even on the same date: October 6, 1805.[2]

The "home parishioners" of Fr. Helbron seemed to have been intermarried with members of the Buffalo mission and some of the latter were without doubt at first members of the Sportsmanshall congregation, but had emigrated during the administration of F. Rogatus Fromm, the predecessor of our missionary. This can be deduced from at least one of his baptisms in Sportsmanshall, viz: entering as sponsors Christian and Mag-

[1] The three entries, Margaret, John and Bridget Hagen are made twice, likewise the baptism of James Sweeny (Schweeny).

[2] The baptismal register of 1805 (as regards Buffalo) contains about seventy different family names of children baptized and of sponsors. Some of these are still found in that locality viz, Easley, Sweeny, Sheridan, Rogers, McElroy.

dalena Ruffner, *néc Isly* (Easly). The Easlys were
undoubtedly in Westmoreland County before they moved
to the Donegal settlement, part of which was the Buffalo
Mission. On March 9, 1794, F. Rogatus Fromm wrote
to Bishop Carroll from Sportsmanshall: "litteras Tuas
20ᵐᵃ Novembris prioris anni ad me per colonum meum
Casparum Easly missas accepi." This same Caspar Isly
(Easly) is found repeatedly in Fr. Helbron's register
under "Boffalo" and he became one of the collectors of
the funds for the first Church at that place, now St.
Patrick's, Sugar Creek, Armstrong Co. From a letter
of the same missionary to Bishop Carroll, dated Pittsburg, Nov. 1, 1805, it is also evident that this Church
owes its foundation to Fr. Helbron. He writes: "Con-
cerning Mr. Flynn, "est vir nullius resolutionis; he left
me at Boufflo, where the congregation bought a place on
purpose for the priest, which is not prepared yet and will
not so soon be ready to receive the priest. I did all
possibility to encourage the people to prepare it at least
in one year. Therefore I would be very glad if your
Lordship send Mr. Mahony . . . Mr. Flynn went down
the River Ohio perhaps to the monks of La Trappe . . .
He was about five weeks with me without celebrating
and preaching but once. I promised to the faithful in
this *wilderness* to come back again in the year here-
after" . . .

Again on October 22, 1806, he wrote to the same
Ordinary in Baltimore: "I baptized in one journey 120
children[1] . . . there is in Bofflo a place bought by the
Catholics ready to receive a priest, the people promised
me to assist him. Mr. Flynn is gone down the river to

[1] The baptismal register shows from the names entered that Fr.
Helbron traveled first northward (Buffalo and Slippery Rock), stopped
at Pittsburg and then visited the southwesern missions of Pennsylvania
(Washington and Green counties).

8

the Trappists." A third letter on this same subject dated June 16, 1807, gives me the news as regards the first pastor of "Buffalo". He writes: The Rev. Mr. Phelin [Father Lawrence Sylv. Phelan] is gone to Bofflo to take possession of the place for the priest; he was with me and I gave him the best direction and instruction for that country."

These missions beyond the Allegheny in the Indian territory "became shortly afterwards some of the best country parishes of the diocese of Pittsburg. The first bishop of this see, Michael O'Connor, in his first census (1843), records them as follows: Donegal, 1300 souls; Murrinsville, 500; St. Patrick's, formerly known as Buffalo Creek Mission, 1000 . . ."[1]

But with the founding of new parishes in new commercial centres these first congregations beyond the Allegheny have gradually lost their membership and their influence.

---

[1] *Biographical Sketches*, Pittsburg, 1914, page 77, states that according to the best authorities the Rev. Lawrence S. Phelan arrived in Buffalo in 1805. These two letters of Fr. Peter Helbron to his bishop prove that Father Phelan became pastor of the Buffalo Mission during the early part of 1807 and after the "short pastorate" of F. Flinn.

FATHER PETER HELBRON'S GREENSBURG PA. REGISTER

FIRST SERIES, 1799 TO 1802.

Copied from the original book by Rev. Father John, O. S. B., of Saint Vincent's Abbey, Pennsylvania. Translated by Lawrence F. Flick, M. D., LL. D.

Greensburg, Pennsylvania, now the county seat of Westmoreland county, was one of the few places in Pennsylvania during the latter part of the eighteenth century and the beginning of the nineteenth in which Catholics could attend Divine Service and receive the ministrations of religion. How it came to be such a place we do not know ; no doubt in a measure at least, it was through its location. Westmoreland County at that time took in much more territory than it does now and must have been before the home-seeking public quite a good deal. The road across the state from east to west went near Greensburg as did also the road from the south to the northwest. The land there is quite fertile and the country is most beautiful so that one can readily understand why people seeking homes would locate there.

Many Catholics from Ireland and Germany and a few from France settled round about Greensburg and within an area of one hundred miles around it. Greensburg itself became a station for traveling priests. In 1789 Father Theodore Browers took up his residence there as pastor. He bought a tract of land near Greensburg before leaving Philadelphia and after his arrival there bought another tract known as Sportsman's Hall which has since become the seat of the famous Benedictine

Abbey founded by Abbot Boniface Wimmer, O. S. B., in 1846. Father Browers soon lost his health and had to go back East.

On November 18, 1799, Father Peter Helbron took up his residence at Greensburg. He served on the mission for a number of years and gave it a permanent organization. Father Helbron kept records of his baptisms, marriages and burials, and it is these records which we here publish. Any records that may have been kept by men preceding him have been lost.

Father Helbron's ministrations took him all over the western part of the State of Pennsylvania and even up into the State of New York. On one occasion he administered the Sacrament of Baptism to thirty-eight people in Buffalo, nearly all children, and on other occasions to large numbers of children in the northwestern and southwestern parts of the state. There is a striking similarity between the names of the people around Greensburg and in western Pennsylvania and the people in Buffalo. It is quite possible that some of the emigrants who went to Westmoreland county went there by way of Buffalo, having followed the water-course from New York over the Hudson and across the lakes to Buffalo and from there by land or possibly even part way by water to the western part of the state.

Father Helbron evidently found much difficulty in properly writing the names of the Irish and sometimes even the Germans and of the French. He spelled names phonetically and sometimes, gave them such odd forms that it is practically impossible to even guess what the original may have been. To aid the reader suggestions of names are put in brackets.

Father Helbron had a definite form for his baptismal entries and usually used it, but sometimes he omitted a word or two. We publish only the salient facts which are of use for genealogical purposes. Those facts are placed in the order which has been followed in our publications heretofore. In a few instances names have been omitted, possibly because they were forgotten, not having been entered immediately. Apparently some of these entries were made from memoranda after returning home from a trip.

A very large number of baptisms on one day as happens in a number of instances would lead one to wonder whether the dates of entry are actually the dates of baptism. On October 22nd, 1803, there were thirty-eight entries of baptisms in Buffalo, some adults and older children but mostly very young children. The gathering together of so large a number of children on a given day in a given place from a scattered population, if all were baptized on the same day, was an extraordinary performance, showing great zeal on the part of both priest and people.

Some of the names which appear in this baptismal record are now found all over the western part of the state of Pennsylvania even much further east than Greensburg, especially up through the Allegheny Mountains, indicating that some of these early settlers or their children or grandchildren must have pushed their way east as well as west. Greensburg seems to have been a distributing point for settlers in all directions.

The original book in which the entries were made has on an average about six entries to the page. On the first page is the inscription:

"Book of Baptisms, Marriages, and Burials beginning with the year 1800 under the Reverend Peter Helbron, Pastor, sent by the Right Reverened Doctor John Carroll, Bishop of Baltimore, and given into his possession by the person in charge of Greensburg in place of the Reverend Mr. Brouers, his lawful and first predecessor on the 17th day of December in the year of Our Lord 1799."

At the top of the second page there is a memorandum saying: "From the year 1799 to the year 1808 there were baptized 578."

Then follow the words: "Baptized after my arrival at Greensburg on the 17th day of November in the Year of Our Lord 1799," and after this the first baptismal entry.

LAWRENCE F. FLICK.

NOTE.—After putting the above introductory to Father Helbron's baptismal register into type, the proof, having been submitted to Father John, O.S.B., fell into the hands of Father Felix Fellner, O.S.B., of St. Vincent Abbey, the historian of the Order. Father Felix, from information at his command, has called attention to some errors in this introductory and has suggested corrections of them. It is deemed preferable to embodying these corrections in the introductory to publish Father Fellner's letter and I hereby append it in a note for this reason.

Dear Doctor:

Father John has asked me to help in the proof-reading of the translated register of E. P. Helbron. This gives me occasion to offer a few suggestions as to the preface to the same register. First, the title, "Father Helbron's Greensburg Register" is misleading.

It is true the title in the original reads Greensburg, but in the letters on hand (copied from Baltimore archives) he writes Sportsmen's Hall near Greensburg (August 1800); or Clear Spring (March 1802) or Clear Spring near Greensburg (August 1808), and only twice is the post-office place of this his church used.

Moreover, the Greensburg congregation *started* a church but never completed it, and finally the project was entirely abandoned. At the same time Father Helbron began the building of the first churches in Pittsburgh, Redstone (Brownsville), Bofflo (Buffalo Creek about thirty to forty miles north of St. Vincent), and Sportsmen's Hall. He wrote, January 30, 1801: "My little chapel which I built here is finished. I blest it in the name of Jesus and

13

entitled it the chapel of the Holy Cross. I intend next spring to repair the other at Greensburg." Or again, March 29, 1802: "My dwelling place shall no more be called Sportsman's Hall but Clear Spring near Greensburg."

Prince Gallitzin lived in *Clearfield* (they were neighbors, and the best of neighbors, as a few letters of Father Helbron's show) and Clear Spring was a literal translation of Helbron (Heller-Brunnen). The name, however, never became popular.

The other difficulty has already been mentioned, viz: Bofflo (Boofflo)–Buffalo. I think the late Father Ganss was the first who applied this Bofflo (Boofflo) to the well-known city in New York State. But this is erroneous. It is true, Father Helbron says in his letters that he travelled to the Indian settlements (Cornplanters) and to the Lakes, but *this* Buffalo applied to a congregation at Buffalo Creek (Armstrong Co., Pennsylvania). This, of course, must change the deductions as to the family names in Greensburg and Buffalo.

The Register of Baptisms 1799.

Gyrven [Girven?], Judith, of Michael and Anna Gyrven, born October 19th, baptized November 18. Sponsors, Daniel and Crescentia Megay [McKay?].

Benson, John, of Jacob and Mary Benson, born February 31st (?), baptized November 25th. Sponsors, George and Sibyla Ruffner.

Thieter, Anna, of Henry, non-Catholic, and Catharine (nee Müller) Catholic, Thieter, born May 14th, baptized November 29th. Sponsors, Anna Mullerin [Mulherin?] widow, and Henry Kuhn, young man.

Wallhy, Mary, of Peter and Mary (nee Gruenewald) Wallhy, born May 9th, baptized December 15th. Sponsors, Joseph and Catharine Schmidt.

Rüffel, Anna Maria, of Bernard and Margaret (nee Diffental) Rüffel, born October 3, baptized December 22nd. Sponsors, George and Anna Maria Zendorff.

Register of Baptisms for 1800.

Original book, page 3.

Daugerthy [Dougherty], Bernard, of Samuel and Sara (nee Kagen) Daugerthy, born February 13th of the preceding year, baptized January 5th. Sponsors, Bernard Riffel and Mary Zendorff.

Mechin [McKean or Maginn?], James, of John and Maxherin (nee Gemmel) Mechin, born May 5th, baptized May 22nd. Sponsors, Peter Roger and Bridget his daughter.

Ruffner, Christian, of George and Sibylla Ruffner, born March 26th, baptized June 1st. Sponsors, Christian Ruffner and Magdalen Isly [Easly?].

14

Ruffner, Anna Maria, of Christian and Margaret Ruffner, born February 21st, baptized June 1st. Sponsors, George and Anna Maria Ruffner.

Curry, Bridget, of John and Margaret (nee Kohl) Curry, born in December (date not given), baptized June 1st. Sponsors, Anthony Rogers and Catharine his mother.

Isly [Easly?], Martha, of Ferdinand and Margaret (nee Meiler) Isly, born April 6th, baptized June 14th. Sponsors, Margaret Mecatery and Henry Meccenhenny [McAnany?].

Original book, page 4.

Preys [Preuss?] Sophie, of Richard and Theresa (nee Kally [Kelly?]) Preys, one year old, baptized June 15th. Sponsors, John Donagy and Cecilia Rogers.

Preys [Preuss?], Rose, of Richard and Theresa (nee Kally [Kelly?]) Preys, three years old, baptized June 15th. Sponsor, John Mehann [Meehan?] and Mary Kammell [Campbell?].

Haygethy [Hagerty], Anna, in the neighborhood of Jacob's Greec [creek] in Fayett [Fayette?] County, formerly a Methodist, with one of her offspring, Margaret, six months old, daughter of Thomas Haygethy. Sponsors, John and Mary Calcher [Gallagher?].

Galcher [Gallagher?], Frances, of John and Mary Galcher, born on the 30th of December of the past year, baptized July 6th. Sponsors, Thomas Haygerthy [Hagerty?] and Bridget Beil [Boyle?].

Beyl [Boyle?], Julia, of Daniel and Julia Beyl, born February 6th, baptized July 6th. Sponsors, Jacob Car [Carr?] and Margaret Mekui [McHugh?].

Galger [Gallagher?], Catharine, of Nicholas Galger (mother's name omitted), born February 8th of the preceding year, baptized July 6th. Sponsors, Anthony Galger and Catharine Car.

Dogen [Dugan?], Crescentia, of Dionysius and Catharine Dogan, seven months old, baptized July 6th. Sponsors, John and Margaret Myccuy [McHugh?].

Original book, page 5.

Mesen [Mason?], Dionysius, of James and Sara Mesen, six months old, baptized July 6th. Sponsors, James and Amelia Car.

Noel, Adam, of Joseph and Margaret (nee Griffin) Noel, born June 11th, baptized July 6th. Sponsors, George and Margaret Ruffner.

Heins, Bernard, of Bernard and Jacobina Heins, born January 7th, baptized July 27th. Sponsors, Bernard Rogers and Cecilia his sister.

Conner, Elizabeth, of Thadeus and Helen (nee Mecalay [McCauley]) Conner, born July 25, baptized August 10. Sponsors, Eva Cammel [Campbell?] and Peter Rogers.

15

Morry [Murray?], William, of James and Anna (nee Schwenny [Sweeney?]) Morry, born May 1st, baptized August 17th. Sponsors, Anthony Rogers and Bridget his sister.

Minhy [Meaney?], Catharine, of James and Mary Minhy, born June 12th, baptized August 31st. Sponsors, Salome Conner and Daniel her brother.

Original book, page 6.

Noel, Peter, of Peter and Margaret Noel, born May 10th, baptized September 7th. Sponsors, Patrick and Margaret Griffing [Griffin?].

Macosca [McCusker?], Regina, of John and Margaret (nee Machschorly [MacSorly?]) Macosca, born March 18th, baptized September 14th. Sponsors, Patrick and Margaret Griffin.

Macosca [McCusker?], James, of John and Margaret Macosca, three years old, baptized September 14th. Sponsors, Francis Galygar [Gallagher?] and Mary Conner.

Garlen [Carlin?], Thomas, of John and Anna Garlen, two years old, baptized September 28th. Sponsors, Peter and Catharine Rogers.

Garlen [Carlin?] Mary, of John and Anna Garlen, born April 10th, baptized September 28th. Sponsors, Bernard Rogers and Catharine Mcqueyny [McQueeney?]

Squeny [Sweeney?] Petronilla, of Carly and Mary Squeny, born March 6th, baptized October 12th. Sponsors, William and Frances Press [Preuss?]

Press [Preuss?] Thomas, of William and Frances Press, born March 6th, 1798, baptized October 12th. Sponsors, Richard Press and Mary Squiny.

Original book page 7.

Conner, Catharine, of Thomas and Magdalen Conner, three years old, baptized October 23rd. Sponsors, Mary Walhy and Henry Kuhn.

Isly [Easly?] John Henry, of Andrew and Elizabeth Isly, born January 2nd, baptized November 2nd. Sponsors, Henry Kuhn and Margaret his wife.

Isly, [Easly?] John Christian, of Caspar and Elizabeth Isly, born October 30, '99, baptized November 2nd. Sponsors, Christian and Magdalen Ruffner.

Meccu [McHugh?] Anna Catharine, of Charles and Anna (nee Laverty [Lafferty?]) Meccu, born on the 21st of the preceding year (month not given), baptized November 21st. Sponsors, Catharine Broun [Brown?] and Henry Kuhn.

Seyvert [Seybert?] Henry, of Philip and Catharine Seyvert, born October 30th, baptized December 8th. Sponsors, Henry and Catharine Kuhn.

Daugherty [Dougherty?] John, of Samuel and Sara Daugherty, (date of birth not given) baptized December 8th. Sponsors, Francis Calger [Gallagher?] and Mary Conner, maiden.

Handly, Mary Anne, of Dionysius and Catharine Handly, born November 1st, baptized December 25th. Sponsors, George and Mary Ruffner.

Mekeneny [McAnany?] Peter, of Henry and Margaret Mekeneny, born December 30th, (evidently of the preceding year) baptized December 25th. Sponsors, Ferdinand and Margaret Isly [Easly?]

REGISTER OF BAPTISMS FOR 1801.

Thresy, [Tracy?] Frank Peter, of Frank and Mary (nee Rogers) Thresy, born February 8th, baptized March 29th. Sponsors, Peter Rogers and Joanna Mecknenning [McAnany].

Alfey [Halvey?] Genevieve, of Patrick and Anna Alfey, born January 28th, baptized May 3rd. Sponsors, Jacob Leth and Anna his wife.

Leth, Mary, of Jacob and Anna Leth, born February 15th, baptized May 3rd. Sponsors, James and Susan Carr.

McBriad [McBride?], Francis, of Neal and Christina McBriad, born October 7th, baptized May 3rd. Sponsors, Patrick Carr and Helen Dugen [Dugan?].

Carr, Susan, of Manasses and Catharine Carr, born July 15th, (evidently of the preceding year but the year is not given), baptized May 3rd. Sponsors, Neal and Crescentia McBraid [McBride?].

Carr, Margaret, of Charles and Anna Carr, born on the 25th, (month not given), baptized May 3rd. Sponsors, Dionysius and Catharine Duggen [Dugan?].

Kirven, John, of Michael and Susan Kirven, born May 1st, baptized May 17th. Sponsors, Manasses O'Donnel and Bridget Rogers.

Kirven, Daniel, of Michael and Susan Kirven, born May 1st, baptized May 17th. Sponsors, Anthony Rogers and Bridget Schorchy [Sharkey?].

Septer, Elizabeth, of Adam and Mary Septer, born April 19th, baptized June 7th. Sponsors, Patrick and Margaret Griffin.

Ruffner, Elizabeth, of Christian and Margaret Ruffner, born May 11th, baptized June 14th. Sponsors, Henry and Margaret Kuhn.

Makelrey [McElroy or McCallery?], Margaret, of Julius and Margaret (nee Gelasby [Gillespie?]) Makelrey, born March 17th, baptized June 19th. Sponsors, Manasses O'Donnel and Anna Coll, maiden.

Dieder, Margaret, of Henry and Catharine Dieder, born May 4th, baptized June 21st. Sponsors, George Kuhn and Margaret Müller, maiden. (See entry of November 29th, 1799, where the name is spelled Thieter).

Doff [Duff?], Frank, of Frank and Anna Doff, born June 2nd, baptized July 26th. Sponsors, Peter Noel and Anna Rogers.

17

Meckelwe [McKelvey?], Mary, of Patrick and Anna Meckelwe, born March 25th '98, baptized August 2nd. Sponsors, Peter Rogers and Annabel Cull. (See entry of June 19th, where occurs the name Anna Coll).

Meckever [McKeever?], Anna, of Patrick and Anna Meckever, born on the 22nd, (month not given) 1801, baptized August 2nd. Sponsors, Anthony Rogers and his sister Bridget.

Hollen, Rose, of· William and Rose Hollen, born March 16th, baptized August 23. Sponsors, Henry Meckenenny [McAanany] and Mary Wallhy.

Dagethy [Dougherty?] James, of James and Anna Dagethy, born the 12th of the same (probably of the previous year), baptized September 6. Sponsors, Manasses O'Donnel and Bridget Schorthy.

Dagethy [Dougherty?], Patrick, of James and Anna Dagethy, two years old, baptized September 6. Sponsors, Frank Thresy [Tracy?] and Cecelia Rogers.

Mihenny [Meaney?] Mary, of John and Margaret Mihenny, born April 17th, baptized September 6th. Sponsors Connel O'Donnel and Margaret his wife.

Gryffen [Griffin?] Elizabeth, of Henry and Magdalen (nee Ruffner) Gryffen, born October 11th, baptized November 1st. Sponsors, Christian and Magdalen (nee Isly [Easly?]) Ruffner.

Aaron [Ahern?] George, of Thomas and Elizabeth Aaron, born September 9th, baptized November 1st. Sponsors, George Ruffner and Mary Braun [Brown?]

Ruffner, Simon, of George and Sibylla Ruffner, born October 3rd, baptized November 1st. Sponsors, Simon and Catharine Ruffner.

——, Thomas, three years old, baptized November 5th. Sponsors, Simon Ruffner and Catharine Braun [Brown?] widow.

Calager [Gallagher?] Julia, of O'Neal and Anna (nee Car [Carr?]) Calager, born June 2, baptized November 8th. Sponsors, O'Neal (christian name not given) and Crofey his wife.

Meckferling [McFarlane?] Daniel, of Meckferling (name of mother omitted, undoubtedly by accident as the child is declared to be the lawful son) eighteen months old, baptized November 8th. Sponsors, James and Nellie Car [Carr?].

Victor, John, of John and Mary Victor, a year old, baptized November 8th. Sponsors, Michael Meckfy [McVey?] and Elizabeth Victor.

Croffey, Mary, of John and Margaret Croffey, born July 7th, baptized November 8th. Sponsors, Daniel Beyl [Boyle?] and his wife.

Meckfy [McVey?] John, of Patrick and Anne Meckfy, born March 13th, '99, baptized November 9th. Sponsors, Neal Meclansy [McGlinchy?] and Margaret Meckuy [McHugh?].

Meckfy [McVey?] Mary, of Patrick and Anna Meckfy, (date of birth not given) baptized, November 9th. Sponsors, Michael Boyl and Isabel Meckuy [McHugh?].

REGISTER OF BAPTISMS FOR 1802.

Brik [Brick or Brück?] Mary, of Henry and Elizabeth Brik, born January 1st, baptized January 31st. Sponsors, George Ruffner and Mary Brik, maiden.

Original book, page 12.

Machin [Maginn?] Anna, of Berny and Salome Machin, born Nov. 4th (probably of the preceding year), baptized February 14th. Sponsors, Catharine and Peter Rogers.

Grünewald, Henry, of Joseph and Mary Ann Grünewald, born January 1st, baptized February 21st. Sponsors, Henry and Margaret Kuhn.

Curry, Catharine, of John and Margaret (nee Cohl [Cole or Kohl?]) Curry, born February 11th, baptized March 14th. Sponsors, Catharine Wallhy and Henry Kuhn, a youth.

Noel, George, of Joseph and Margaret Noel, born March 16th, baptized March 22nd. Sponsors, Patrick and Margaret Griffy [Greavey?].

Septer, Henry, of Frederick and Mary Septer, seven years old, baptized March 23rd. Sponsors, Patrick and Margaret Griffy [Greavey?].

Septer, Susan, of Frederick and Mary Septer, three years old, baptized March 23rd. Sponsors, Patrick and Margaret Griffy [Greavey?].

Septer, Mary Ann, of Frederick and Mary Septer, born January 27th, baptized March 23rd. Sponsors, Joseph Noel and Catharine Ruffner wife of Simon Ruffner.

Wallhy, Nicholas, of Peter and Mary Wallhy, born January 17th, baptized April 4th. Sponsors, Nicholas Wallhy and Elizabeth Schmidt.

Original book, page 13.

Allwein, Catharine, of Jacob and Catharine Allwein, born January 3rd, baptized April 11th. Sponsors, Joseph and Catharine Schmidt.

Peyfer [Pfeiffer?], George, of George and Anna Maria Peyfer, born July 19th (probably of the preceding year), baptized April 18th. Sponsors, Martin Müller and Margaret his sister both unmarried.

Morry [Murray?], John, of James and Ann Morry, born March 2nd, baptized May 6th. Sponsors, Connel O'Donnel and Bridget his daughter.

Noel, Susan, of Peter and Margaret Noel, born September 15th, baptized May 8th. Sponsors, Nicholas Wallhy and Mary his wife. (The two entries of May 6th and 8th are apparently interjected into the April record of baptisms.)

Dolen [Dolan?], Thomas, of Michael and Margaret Dolen, born June 9th, baptized April 25th. Sponsors, Patrick May and Elizabeth Rogen [Rogan?].

19

Roger, Rose, of Frank and Elizabeth Roger, born December 19th, (evidently of the preceding year), baptized April 25th. Sponsors, Jacob Brauer and Mary Monteck [Montague?].

Dogcarthy [Dougherty?], Sara, of James and Isabel Dogcarthy, born December 6th (evidently of the preceding year), baptized April 25th. Sponsors, Daniel and Mary Dogcarthy.

Gallager [Gallagher?] Daniel, of James and Anna Gallager, born March 1st, baptized April 25th. Sponsors, Manasses and Catharine Roger.

Mcguy [McGee?] Susan, of William and Elizabeth Mcguy, born December 22nd, baptized April 29th. Sponsors, Jacob May and Catharine Clerick.

Original book, page 14.

Clerick, Daniel, of Jacob and Mary Clerick, born January 5th, baptized April 29th. Sponsors, John Ketter and Mary, maiden.

Clerick, Daniel, of Daniel and Sara Clerick, born October 16th, (evidently of the preceding year) baptized April 29th. Sponsors, James and Isabel Schuy [Shea?].

Reily, Charity, of James and Cecilia Reily, born September 25th, (evidently of the preceding year), baptized April 29th. Sponsors, William McKaen [McCann?] and Charity Dannly [Donnelly?].

Dannly [Donnelly?] Isabel of Felix and Charity Dannly, born March 8th, baptized April 29th. Sponsors, Thomas and Anna McKann [McCann?]

Gelasby [Gillespie?] Mary Ann, of Neal Gelasby, Jr. and Thamar his wife, born May 21st, (probably the preceding year) baptized May 2nd. Sponsors, Neal Gelasby Sr., and Susan Gilasby.

Menny, [Meaney?] Edward, of Edward Menny (name of mother omitted), born May 21st (evidently of the previous year), baptized May 2nd. Sponsors Emmanuel Born and Mary Trugs.

Therner [Turner?] Martin, of Martin and Mary Therner, born March 26th, baptized May 2nd. Sponsors, James Dagarthy [Dougherty?] and Mary Mecloden.

Dagarthy [Dougherty?] James, of James and Catharine Dagarthy, born March 1st, 1801, baptized May 2nd. Sponsors, Martin and Mary Therner [Turner?].

Creny Edward, of John and Elizabeth Creny, born September 16th, 1800, baptized May 2nd. Sponsors, Edward Mcschary [McSherry?] and Susan Drugs.

Therrer [Turner?] Catharine, of Thady and Elizabeth Therrer, born March 19th, 1801, baptized May 2nd. Sponsors, Michael Therrer and Susan Trugs.

Quickly, [Quigley?] William, of William and Sara Quickly, born September 8th, (evidently of the previous year) baptized May 2nd. Sponsors, Bernard Bressly and Mary Borne.

20

Dagerthy [Dougherty?] William, of William and Margaret Dagerthy, born March 14th, baptized May 30th. Sponsors, Dionysius Conner and Bridget Rogers.

Heins, Jacob, of Bernard and Helen Heins, born January 13th, baptized May 30th. Sponsors, George Ruffner and his daughter Catharine.

Deffeling, Jacob, of Leonard and Sara Deffeling, born October 13th, 1801, baptized June 6th. Sponsors, Daniel O'Donnel and Cecilia Rogers.

Wenny, Dionysius, of Charles and Mary (nee Griffy [Greavey?]) Wenny, born April 8th, baptized June 6th. Sponsors, Frank Thomsy [Dempsey?] and Catharine Rogers.

Gely [Gayley?] Patrick, of Patrick and Margaret Gely, born June 26th, 1801, baptized. June 20th. Sponsors, Joseph Grunewald and Mary Ann.

Press [Preuss?] Frances, of William and Frances Press, born June 17th, 1801, baptized June 20th. Sponsors, John and Margaret Michaen [McKean?]

O'Donnel, Mary Ann, of Connel and Margaret O'Donnel, born May 27th, baptized June 20th. Sponsors, Timothy Connor and Margaret his daughter.

Ruffner, Johanna Simon, of Simon and Mary Barbara Ruffner, born May 19th, baptized August 22nd. Sponsors, John Henry and Barbara Ruffner, maiden.

Septer, Mary, of Adam and Mary Septer, born June 5th, baptized August 29th. Sponsors, Frederick and Mary Septer.

McGlochen [McLoughlin?] John, of William and Catharine McLochen, born January 31st, baptized August 29th. Sponsors, Connel O'Donnel and Margaret Corry [Curry?].

Daugethy, [Dougherty?] Catharine, of —— (Christian name of father not given) and Salome Daughety, born July 24th, baptized August 6th. Sponsors, Bridget O'Donnel and Daniel O'Donner.

Denny, John, of Dionysius and Unita Denny, born July 14th, baptized August 6th. Sponsors, Manasses O'Donnel and Cecilia Rogers.

Ruffner, Catharine, of Christian and Margaret Ruffner, born June 14th, baptized September 19th. Sponsors, George Ruffner, bachelor and Mary Kuhn, maiden.

Conner, Graffert, of William and Susan Conner, born May 28th, of the preceding year, baptized October 3rd. Sponsors, Nicholas and Catharine Darby.

Mony [Mooney?] Margaret, of William and Mary (nee Collen [Collins?]) Mony, born July 19th, baptized October 10th. Sponsors, John Pollin and Bridget Rogers.

Cambell [Campbell?], John, of Philip and Mary (nee Megey [Magee or McKay?]) Cambell, born March 11th, baptized October 10th. Sponsors, Daniel O'Donnel and Cecilia Rogers.

Original book, page 17.

Mony [Mooney?], John, of William and Mary (nee Coller) Mony, born June 11th, baptized October 10th. Sponsors, Philip Cambell [Campbell?] and Mary Megoy [McCoy?].

Coller, George, of John and Catharine Coller, born November 25th, baptized October 15th. Sponsors, George and Anna Mary Ruffner.

——, Salome Theresa, daughter of unknown mother, three years old, baptized October 15th. Sponsors, Salome and John Kelley her husband, they adopting the little girl.

Lany, Jacob, of Jacob and Mary Lany, born August 4th, baptized November 8th. Sponsors, Peter Declara and Margaret Meccferly.

Kaffee [Caffrey?], James, of James and Margaret Kaffee, born October 1st, baptized November 8th. Sponsors, Dionysius and Margaret Morphy [Murphy?].

Declara, John, of Peter and Catharine Declara, born November 4th, 1801, baptized November 9th. Sponsors, Anthony Constantine De Belen and Mary Morphy [Murphy?] widow.

De Belan, Mary Theresa, of Anthony Constantine and Elizabeth De Belan, born March 31st, baptized November 9th. Sponsors, Ludwig de Walleur and Mary Julia Berthow, maiden. (The name Walleur here is probably the same as Wallhy and Wallly which have been encountered before. It is apparently a French name which in previous entries may have been spelled phonetically*).

* Father Felix Fellner O. S. B. calls attention to the fact that Wallhy lived near Sportman's Hall whilst de Walleur lived in Pittsburgh.

——, John, son of Theegarden, twenty-seven years old, who heretofore had professed no religion. Baptized November 13th. Sponsors, John and Rose Meguire [McGuire?].

Original book, page 18.

Collerick, Henry, of John and Ann Collerick, born August 2nd, baptized November 13th. Sponsors, John Collerick and Mary Collerick, maiden.

Carlaan [Callahan?], Eleanor, of Edward and Julia Carlaan, born July 8th, baptized Nov. 14th. Sponsors, Michael Brannen and Cecilia Rogen.

McCaen [McCann?], James, of Daniel and Ann McCaen, born March 29th, baptized November 14th. Sponsors, Julius Brannen and Elizabeth Twettell.

Roger, John, of Frank and Elizabeth Roger, born April 6th, baptized November 14th. Sponsors, Henry and Rose Montecc [Montague?].

Beyl [Boyle?], John, of Felix and Ann Beyl, born April 1st, baptized November 21st. Sponsors, John and Margaret Mollrain [Mulherin?].

Michen [Meehan or McKean?], John, of William and Elizabeth Michen, born October 22nd, baptized November 21st. Sponsors, Felix and Ann Beyl [Boyle?].

Mecady [McCarthy?], Bernard, of Patrick and Elizabeth Mecady, born February 6th, baptized November 21st. Sponsors, John Reis [Rice?] and Susan Gelaspy [Gillespie?].

Clerin, Elizabeth, of John and Helen Clerin, born March 16th, baptized November 21st. Sponsors, Thomas Kühn and his sister Anna.

Dagerthy [Dougherty?], James, of James and Anne Dagerthy, born September 21st, baptized November 21st. Sponsors, James Dagarthy and Ann Mellbosch.

Dagarthy [Dougherty?], Thomas, of Daniel and Ann Dagarthy, born May 9th, baptized November 21st. Sponsors, John and Ann Collerick.

Original book, page 19.

Wabold, Ann, of Luke and Margaret Wabold, born September 16th, 1800, baptized November 24th. Sponsors, Neal Gelaspy [Gillespie?] and his sister Susan.

Wabold, Susan, of Luke and Margaret Wabold, born June 21st, baptized November 24th. Sponsors, John Kilgen and Susan wife of Gelaspy.

Meccfergin, Edward, of . . . and Catharine Meccfergin (christian name of the father not given), born July 27th, baptized November 28th. Sponsors, Charles and Helen Meccfergin.

Car [Carr?], Anna, of Mannasses and Catharine Car, born June 13th, baptized November 28th. Sponsors, Daniel Brogen and Bridget Ahlon [Allen?].

Car [Carr?], Frances, of Patrick and Petronilla Car, born October 19th, baptized November 28th. Sponsors, James Meganey and Helen Dugen [Dugan?].

Dugen [Dugan?], Bridget, of Daniel and Catharine Dugen, born May 22nd, baptized November 28th. Sponsors, James and Catharine Car.

Leonard, Jacob, of Jacob and Rachel Leonard, born July 7th, baptized November 28th. Sponsors. Bernard Hueckens [Higgins?] and Catharine his sister.

Meccferling, [McFarlane?] Edward, of Edward and Catharine Meccferling (date of birth not given), baptized November 28th. Sponsors, Daniel Beyl [Boyle?]. (Although the word sponsors is used, only one is given.)

23

FATHER PETER HELBRON'S GREENSBURG PA. REGISTER

Copied from the original book by Rev. Father John, O. S. B., of
Saint Vincent's Abbey, Pennsylvania. Translated by Lawrence F.
Flick, M. D., LL. D.

REGISTER OF BAPTISMS FOR 1803.

Hendell, Salome, of Daniel and Catharine Hendell, born December
2nd, baptized February 13th. Sponsors, Bridget O' Donnell and
Henry Kuhn.

Original book, page 20.

Flouer, Henry, of Henry and Margaret Flouer (date of birth not
given), baptized March 16th. Sponsors, Joseph Flouer and his wife.

Flouer, Joseph, of Joseph and Catharine Flouer (date of birth not
given), baptized March 16. Sponsors, Henry Flouer and his wife.

Flouer, Thomas and Margaret, of Thomas and Elizabeth Flouer (date
of birth not given), baptized March 16th. Sponsors, Joseph Flouer
and his wife.

O'Bryen, [O'Brien?] Mary Susan and Rose, of Daniel and Mary
O'Bryen (date of birth not given), baptized March 16th. Sponsors, relatives whose names are not known. (Whilst the word
"ignota" is used, the meaning evidently is "have been forgotten.")

Keyl, [Kyle?] Catharine, of Philip and Catharine Keyl, born October
12th, (evidently of preceding year), baptized March 26th. Sponsors, Andrew and Catharine Champbell [Campbell?].

Cannovy, Samuel, of Samuel and Patience Cannovy, born December
21st, (evidently of preceding year), baptized March 26th. Sponsors,
Michael and Margaret Champbell [Campbell?] unmarried.

Isly, [Easly?] Elizabeth, of Andrew and Elizabeth Isly, born March
17th, baptized April 10th. Sponsors, Henry Kuhn and his sister
Mary.

Zindorff, Peter, of George and Anna Mary Zindorff, born October
12th (evidently of preceding year), baptized April 24. Sponsors,
John Noele and Mary Kuhn.

Original book, page 21.

Lochler, Jacob, of John and Margaret Lochler, born May 1st, 1802,
baptized May 3rd. Sponsors, James Meckfall [McFaul?] and Helen
Lory [Lowry?].

Weith, [White?] Susan, of Joseph and Mary Weith, born December 18th, 1802, baptized May 3rd. Sponsors, John Lochley and Catharine Meckfall [McFaul?].

Yeaman, Jacob, of Jacob and Helen Yeaman (date of birth not, given), baptized May 3rd. Sponsors, Patrick Brannen and Mary Morphy [Murphy?].

Hammell, Catharine, of Patrick and Mary Hammell, born May 30th, 1802, baptized May 3rd. Sponsors, Michael and Elizabeth Martinimy.

Numen [Newman?], Mary Ann, of Peter and Margaret Numen, ten years old, baptized May 4th. Sponsors, Patrick and Mary Numen.

Lery [Leary?], Helen, of William and Mary Lery, four years old, baptized May 4th. Sponsors, John Meckfall [McFaul?] and Julia Carder [Carter?].

Schleth, Edward, of Daniel and Margaret Schleth, born May 2nd, 1802, baptized May 4th. Sponsors, Anthony Kelly and Margaret Numen [Newman?].

Braun, [Brown?], George, of James aud Frances Braun, born July 16th, 1802, baptized May 9th. Sponsors, James Dageurthy [Dougherty?] and Rose Mantecka.

Dageurthy [Dougherty?], Sara, of William and Margaret Dageurthy, born April 6, 1802, baptized May 9th. Sponsors, John Cannedy [Kennedy?] and Margaret Finck.

Thernan [Tiernan?], Mary, of Patrick and Margaret Thernan, born August 9th, 1802, baptized May 15th. Sponsors, Amund Borne and Susan Gelaspy [Gillespie?].

Kühn, Elizabeth, of John and Mary Kühn, born December 6th, 1803, (evidently a mistake for 1802) baptized May 15th. Sponsors, John Mollery [Mulherin?] and Margaret his wife.

Dageurthy [Dougherty?], John, of James and Catharine Dageurthy, born January 12th, baptized May 15th. Sponsors, John Dageurthy and Susan.

Delany, Mary Ann, of Dionysius and Margaret Delany, born February 27th, 1802, baptized May 15th. Sponsors, John Meclany [McIlhenny?] and Mary Dagourthy [Dougherty?].

Original book, page 22.

Meckerr [McGirr?], William, of John and Petronilla Meckerr, born October 22nd (evidently of preceding year), baptized May 15th. Sponsors, Patrick Lies and Margaret Delany.

Gelaspy [Gillespie?], John, of James and Mary Gelaspy, born February 17th, 1802, baptized May 16th. Sponsors, Patrick and Margaret Thernan [Tiernan?].

Gelaspy [Gillespie?], Elizabeth, of James and Mary Gelaspy, born January 6th, 1800, baptized May 16th. Sponsors, Michael Thernan [Tiernan?] and Susan Gelaspy.

25

Meccshery [McSherry?] Bartholomew, of Angus and Isabel Mecc-Shery, born November 22nd 1802, baptized May 16th. Sponsors, Bartholomew Meccschery and Mary Thernan [Tiernan?].

Therrens [Torrance?] Charles, of Michael and Elizabeth Therrens, born April 13, 1803, baptized May 16th. Sponsors, John and Margaret Dagourthy [Dougherty?].

Beckery, Mary Susan, of —— Beckery (Christian name of father not given) and Frances his wife, of no religion, sixteen years old, baptized May 22nd. Sponsor, Prudence Derbyn [Durbin?].

Beyl, [Boyle?] Genevieve, of Daniel and Genevieve Beyl, born May 1st, 1803, baptized May 22nd. Sponsors, Charles and Catharine Harken.

Galegar [Gallagher?] Margaret, of Anthony and Bridget Galegar, born February 20th, 1802, baptized May 22nd. Sponsors, Patrick Beyl [Boyle?] and Elizabeth Meckuy [McHugh?].

Car [Carr?] Bridget, of Charles and Mary Ann Car, born February 15, 1802, baptized May 22nd. Sponsors, Dionysius and Catharine Dugen [Dugan?].

Galegar [Gallagher?] Mary, of John and Mary Galegar, born March 22, 1803, baptized May 22nd. Sponsors, Bernard Harken and Petronilla Dugen [Dugan?].

Easten [Easton?] Mary, of George and Barbara Easten, twelve years old, baptized May 22nd, sponsors, Nicholas Meclansy and Elizabeth Singery.

Singery, Jacob, of Thomas and Elizabeth Singery, six years old, baptized May 22nd. Sponsors, Nicholas Meclansy. (The plural word sponsors is used, but only one sponsor is given.)

Singery, Thomas, of Thomas and Elizabeth Singery, three years old, baptized May 22nd. Sponsors, Julius Beyl [Boyle?] and Catharine Galeghar [Gallagher?]

Original book, page 23.

Fincher, Charles, of Thomas and Elizabeth Fincher, born September 6th, baptized May 22nd. Sponsors, Michael Meckuy [McHugh?] and Mary Harken.

Brick, George, of Peter and Margaret Brick, born April 22nd, baptized May 29th. Sponsors, George and Anna Mary Ruffner.

Seyvert [Seybert?] John, of Philip and Mary Seyvert, born April 19th, baptized May 29th. Sponsors, Thomas and Elizabeth Aaron [Ahern?]

Adschar, Peter, of John and Elizabeth Adschar, five years old, baptized May 29th. Sponsors, Peter Koss and Theresa Brick.

Griffy [Greavy?] George, of Henry and Magdalen Griffy, born April 28th, baptized June 12th. Sponsors, Joseph Noel and Mary Ruffner, maiden.

Ruffner . . . (no christian name of Child given) daughter of George and Sybilla Ruffner, born May 8th, baptized June 12th. Sponsors, George and Elizabeth Ruffner.

Schorthy, Bridget, of Juy and Elizabeth Schorthy, born April 29th, baptized June 12th. Sponsors, Peter Rogers and Catharine his wife.

——, (no surname given) Peter, thirteen years old, deserted by parents, baptized August 28th. Sponsors, John and Martha Mecavy.

Original book, page 24.

Isly [Easly?] Peter Ferdinand, of Ferdinand and Margaret Isly, born July 31st, baptized August 28th. Sponsors, Christian and Magdalen Ruffner.

Merckell, [Markle?] John, of John and Barbara Merckell, born September 7th, baptized October 9th. Sponsors, Jacob Kuhn and Mary Henry, maiden.

(After this entry is inserted a note) "In a visit made to all the stations in the new territory on the other side of the Allegeny [Allegheny] and Monocohely [Monongahela] Rivers."

McKellway, Anna, of Patrick and Anna McKellway, born August 17th, baptized October 11th. Sponsors, John and Margaret Schmidt.

Dagourthy, [Dougherty?] Sara, of Patrick and Ann Dagourthy (date of birth is not given), baptized October 11th. Sponsors, Patrick Mckellway and his daughter Margaret.

Meckderrly, Anna, of Cornelius and Mary Meckderrly, one year old, baptized October 12th. Sponsors, Patrick Ferry and Bridget Meckbraid [McBride?].

Meckbraid [McBride] Bridget, of Patrick and Bridget Meckbraid, born April 3rd, baptized October 16th. Sponsors, Cornelius and Mary Meckferry.

Kohl, Jacob, of Peter and Catharine Kohl, born February 27, baptized October 16th. Sponsors, Juy and Elizabeth Schorthy.

Lill [Lilly?] Frank, of James and Elizabeth Lill, born March 25th, baptized October 16th. Sponsors, Peter and Catharine Kohl.

Begen, John, of Patrick and Margaret Begen, born June 30th, baptized October 16th. Sponsors, James and Elizabeth Lill [Lilly?].

Meckelly, Bridget, of William and Catharine Meckelly, born December 8th, (no doubt of the preceding year), baptized October 16th. Sponsors, Gelaspy and his wife. [Gillespie?]

Roger, Peter, of Jonas and Cecilia Roger, born February 5th, baptized October 16th. Sponsors, John and Catharine Morren.

Original book, page 25.

Carry [Carey?] Joseph of Michael and Margaret Carry, born December 29th (no doubt of preceding year), baptized October 16th. Sponsors, Joseph Morren and Judith Kelly.

Meckenolly, [McAnally?] Julius, of Patrick and Mary Meckenolly,

27

born December 20th (evidently of preceding year), baptized October 16th. Sponsors, James Morren and Catharine Meckenolly.

Schorthy, Mary of Anthony and Bridget Schorthy, born March 28th, baptized October 16th. Sponsors, John and Anna Wellreck.

Kreen, [Green?] Catharine, of James and Genevieve Kreen, born March 22, baptized October 16th. Sponsors, Bridget and Anthony Schorthy.

Meckuy [McHugh?] Rose, of Joseph and Mary Meckuy, born September 27th, baptized October 16th. Sponsors, Edward and Judith Kohl.

Meckenelly, [McAnally?] George, of —— (Christian name of father not given) and Mary Meckenelly, born —— 27th (month not given), baptized October 16th. Sponsors, John and Margaret Schmidt.

Schmidt, Catharine, of John and Margaret Schmidt, born June 14th, baptized October 16th. Sponsors, Michael and Mary Welsch.

Grahm [Graham?] Sara, of James and Genevieve Grahm, born May 14th, baptized October 16th. Sponsors, Edward and Margaret Meckferrly.

(Note here states). All of those just going before were baptized at Schlypery [Slippery?] Rock.

Rogers, Bernard, of Cornelius and Anne Rogers, born April 18, 1802, baptized October 22nd. Sponsors, John Dugen [Dugan?] and Catharine Forker [Foraker?].

Forker [Foraker?] Bridget, of John and Rose Forker, born May 18, baptized October 22. Sponsors, Cornelius O'Donnel and Bridget Dugen [Dugan?].

Heyl, August, of John and Elizabeth Heyl, born in 1803 (month not given), baptized October 22nd. Sponsors, Cornelius and Ann Roger.

Meclachlen [McLaughlin?] James, of Patrick and Anne Meclachlen, born March 4, 1803, baptized October 22nd. Sponsors, Thomas and Elizabeth Dugen [Dugan?]

Gelaspy [Gillespie?] Manasses, of John and Othelia Gelaspy, born August 15th, 1802, baptized October 22nd. Sponsors, Daniel O'Donnell and Petronilla Kohl.

Original book, page 26.

Anderson, Isaac, of Joseph and Mary Anderson, born May 10, 1803, baptized October 22nd. Sponsors, Charles and Catharine Schwiny [Sweeney?].

Black, John, of Archibald and Regina Black (date of birth not given), baptized October 22nd. Sponsors, Morrall Meclansy and Treys.

Quinn, Daniel, of Joseph and Catharine Quinn, born August 15th, baptized October 22nd. Sponsors, Daniel and Bridget Reed.

Doffy [Duffy?] Barnaby, of John and Sophia Doffy, born September 11th, baptized October 22nd. Sponsors, John and Anna Caleghar [Gallagher?].

Doffy, [Duffy?] Petronilla, of John and Anna Doffy (date of birth not given), baptized October 22nd. Sponsors, Peter and Catharine Dagourthy. [Dougherty?]

Dogourthy [Dougherty?] Anna, of Peter and Anna Dogourthy (date of birth not given), baptized October 22nd. Sponsors, John and Anna Doffy. [Duffy?]

Meckuy [McHugh?] Bridget, of Daniel and Bridget Meckuy, born February 6th, 1802. baptized October 22nd. Sponsors, James and Bridget Meckuy [McHugh?]

McKirley, Catharine, of — (Christian name of father not given) and Bridget McKirley, born May 1st, 1803, baptized October 22nd. Sponsors, Daniel and Bridget Meckuy [McHugh?]

Meckbraid, [McBride?] Margaret, of John and Mary Meckbraid, born May 15th, 1803, baptized October 22nd. Sponsors, John and Margaret McBraid.

Meclay, John, of William and Catharine Meclay, born July 17th, baptized October 22nd. Sponsors, John and Margaret McKirly.

Dorry [Derry?] Salome, of John and Rose Dorry, born March 30th, baptized October 22nd. Sponsors, Peter and Mary McBraid [McBride?].

McBraid [McBride?] Henry, of Patrick and Mary McBraid, born April 12th, baptized October 22nd. Sponsors, Manasses Dugen [Dugan?] and Catharine Dorry [Derry?].

Meckferrly, Edward, of Edward and Anna Meckferrly, born July 27th, baptized October 22nd. Sponsors, Edward and Catharine McKirly.

Kelly, Frank, of Bernard and Bridget Kelly, born March 12th, 1802, baptized October 22nd. Sponsors, Peter and Sophie Farren.

Griffy [Greavy?] George, of John and Mary Griffy, born July 31st, 1803, baptized October 22nd. Sponsors, Philip and Margaret Hartman.

Original book, page 27.

Haegen [Hagen?], James, of Andrew and Margaret Haegen, born September 3rd, 1802, baptized October 22nd. Sponsors, Michael and Mary Keely.

Meckferring, Charles, of Edward and Mary Meckferring, born May 18th, baptized October 22nd. Sponsors, Philip, Meckelrey [McElroy?] and Catharine Green.

Meckohl [McCall?], Elizabeth, of James and Petronilla Meckohl, born April 22, 1801, baptized October 22nd. Sponsors, Terence and Elizabeth McKohl.

Mecherrikell [McGarrigle?], Anna, of James and Anna Mecherrikell,

29

born April 22nd, baptized October 22nd. Sponsors, Patrick and Meckellfy [McKelvey?].

O'Donnell, Sara, of . . . (christian name of father not given) and Mary O'Donnell, born February 7th, baptized October 22. Sponsors, John and Anna Meclachlen McLaughlin?].

Doffy [Duffy?], Michael, of Charles and Nellie Doffy (date of birth not given), baptized October 22. Sponsors, Michael and Margaret Dugen [Dugan?].

Calaghar [Gallagher?], William, of William and Petronilla Calaghar (date of birth not given), baptized October 22nd. Sponsors, Patrick Calaghar and Petronilla O'Donnel.

Christy, Peter, of Archibald and Mary Christy, born July 17, 1802, baptized October 22nd. Sponsors, Andrew and Susan Dugen [Dugan?]·

Ferry, John, of Edward and Margaret Ferry (date of birth not given), baptized October 22nd. Sponsors, Archibald and Mary Christy.

Dugen [Dugan?], Dionysius, of James and Mary Dugen (date of birth nor given), baptized October 22nd. Sponsors, James Schordy and Mary Dorry [Derry?].

Collenz, [Collins?], John, of William and Julia Collenz (date of birth not given), baptized October 22nd. Sponsors, Patrick Lafferty and Elizabeth Harger.

Merhy [Murray?], Bernard, of John and Cecelia Merhy (date of birth nct given), baptized October 22nd. Sponsors, Edward and Mary Ferry.

Original book, page 28.

Collenz [Collins?], Charles, of William and Julia Collenz (date of birth not given), baptized October 22nd. Sponsors, Michael and Theresa Dugen? [Dugan?].

Hargen, Juy, of Robert and Elizabeth Hargen (date of birth not given), baptized October 22nd. Sponsors, Michael and Barbara Doffy [Duffy?].

Collenz [Collins?], William, of William and Julia Collenz (date of birth not given), baptized October 22nd. Sponsors, Bernard Kely [Kelly?] and Petronilla Calaghar [Gallagher?].

Preys, [Preuss?], Genevieve, of Richard and Theresa Preys (date of birth not given), baptized October 22nd. Sponsors, Edward Dagourthy [Dougherty?] and Catharine McBraid [McBride?].

——, Thomas, (date of birth not given), baptized October 22nd. Sponsors, Julius and Julia Mackelrey [McElroy?].

Harkin, Catharine, of Robert and Mary Harkin (date of birth not given), baptized October 22nd. Sponsors, John and Rose Forker [Foraker?].

[Note] all of the above were baptized in Boofflo [Buffalo].

MecKelway, Catharine, of Michael and Elizabeth MecKelway (date of birth not given), baptized November 6th. Sponsors, Patrick Brannen and Martha McKuy [McHugh?].

Numan [Newman?], Petronilla, of Patrick and Eleanor Numan, (date of birth not given), baptized November 6th. Sponsors, Dionysius Morphy [Murphy?] and Catharine McKall [McCall?].

Michen [Meehan?], Genevieve, of James and Mary Michen, (date of birth not given), baptized November 6th. Sponsors, John Brannen and Anna Braun [Brown?].

Michen [Meehan?], William, of James and Mary Michen (date of birth not given), baptized November 6th. (The word sponsors is omitted), Daniel and Eleanor Lachel.

Mecady, Mary, of Edward and Elizabeth Mecady, (date of birth not given), baptized November 6th. Sponsors, David and Elizabeth Dorby [Durby?].

Braun [Brown?], Anne, of John and Anna Braun, (date of birth not given), baptized November 6th. Sponsors, Christopher and Catharine Braun.

Branen [Brannen?], Salome, of John and Anna Branen (date of birth not given), baptized November 6th. Sponsors, James Brannen and Mary Clany.

Original book, page 29.

Müller, Elizabeth, of Jacob and Sara Müller (date of birth not given), baptized November 6th. Sponsors, Dionysius and Unita Denny.

Cany [Kenny?], Helen, of James and Margaret Cany (date of birth not given), baptized November 7th. Sponsors, Anthony Kelly and Helen Nummen [Newman?].

Gud, [Good?] Mary, of Balthasar and Rose Gud, (date of birth not given) baptized, November 7th, (the word sponsors is omitted) Morgen Born and Mary Nummen [Newman?].

Gud [Good?] Frank, of Balthasar and Rose Gud, (date of birth not given), baptized November 7th. Sponsors, Moyse Born and Mary Kelly.

Caleghar [Gallagher?] Jovita, of Michael and Margaret Caleghar (date of birth not given), baptized November 14th. Sponsors, James and Frances Braun [Brown?].

Waith [White?] of James and Elizabeth Waith (date of birth not given), baptized November 14th. Sponsors, Michael Caleghar [Gallagher?] and Elizabeth Waith.

Workman, Elizabeth, of Jacob and Mary Workman (date of birth not given), baptized November 20th. Sponsors, Nicholas and Margaret Gelaspy [Gillespie?].

Meckfuy [McVey?] Margaret, of Patrick and Anna Meckfuy (date of birth not given), baptized November 20th. Sponsors Jacob and Ann Leaden.

Leaden, Anna, of Jacob and Anna Leaden (date of birth not given), baptized November 20th. Sponsors, Patrick and Anna Morphy [Murphy?].

31

Chartery, Helen, of Daniel and Helen Chartery (date of birth not given), baptized November 20th. Sponsors, John Kuhn and Cecilia Realy [Rahilly?].

Mcgady, Mary, of Patrick and Elizabeth Mcgady, (date of birth not given) baptized November 20th. Sponsors, Patrick Goenen [Gannon?] and Catharine Donnely.

Realy [Rahilly?] Elizabeth, of James and Elizabeth Realy (date of birth not given), baptized November 20th. Sponsors, Thomas Kuhn and Salome Guy.

Dagourthy [Dougherty?] Patrick, of John and Susan Dagourthy (date of birth not given), baptized November 20th. Sponsors, James and Anna Dagourthy.

Original book, page 30,

Collman [Coleman?] Anna, of John and Mary Collman (date of birth not given), baptized November 20th. Sponsors, Jacob and Ann Gramenich.

Lily [Lilly?] Nicholas, of George and Elizabeth Lily (date of birth not given), baptized November 20th. Sponsors, John Morris and Catharine Clinger.

Haeffner, Benjamin, about thirty years old, baptized in the presence of the congregation, November 24th. Formerly a Quaker (Queckeranus).

Thresy, [Tracy,] Salome, of Frank and Mary Thresy, (date of birth not given). baptized December 4th. Sponsors, John and Martha Mcgay [McGee?].

Grünewald, Mary, of Joseph and Mary Grünewald, born December 4, baptized December 25th. Sponsors, George Kuhn and Mary Kannenn [Cannon?].

McBraid, [McBride?] Sophie, of Andrew and Mary McBraid, born July 27th, baptized December 25th. Sponsors, Henry Kuhn and Mary Seyfferts. [Seybert?].

(Note) N. B. The three following were baptized on the 27th of November.

Victor, Elizabeth, of John and Mary Victor, four years old, baptized November 27th. Sponsors, Patrick McDarmet [McDermott?] and Elizabeth Victor.

Calaghar [Gallagher?] James, of Adam and Mary Calaghar (date of birth not given) baptized November 27th. Sponsors, Charles and Catharine Hasguyt [Hapgood?].

Doff [Duff?] Mary, of Frank and Mary Doff (date of birth not given) baptized, November 27th. Sponsor, McGuy [McHugh?] (The word for sponsors is abbreviated so it is not possible to tell whether it is singular or plural and only one surname without a Christian name of a person is given).

FATHER PETER HELBRON'S GREENSBURG, PA. REGISTER

Copied from the original book by the Rev. Father John, O. S. B., of Saint Vincent's Abbey, Pennsylvania. Translated by Lawrence F. Flick, M. D., LL. D.

REGISTER OF BIRTHS FOR 1804.

Original book, page 31.

NOTE: Underneath the entry of the year the names of the months of January, March and April are placed. Below these, before the entries, numerals are placed, without, however, indicating which of the three months is meant.

Daugherty, Sara, of Lagely and Sara Daugherty, born March 17, baptized on the 1st. Sponsors, Dionysius Conner and Margaret his sister.

Curring [Curry?], Mary, of John and Margaret Curring, date of birth March 2nd, baptized April 1st. Sponsors, Neil Mcglary and Bridget Shorthy.

Noell, Mary, of John and Petronilla Noell, born in January, baptized the 1st. Sponsors, Frederick Septer and Margaret Griffy.

Müller, John, of Martin and Magdalen Müller, born March 14, baptized the 8th (month not stated). Sponsors, John and Barbara Henrich [Henry?].

Daugerthy, John, of William and Margaret Daugerthy, born March 5th, baptized the 15th (month not stated). Sponsors, George and Sybilla Ruffner.

Brick, Mary, of Henry and Elizabeth Brick, born March 25, baptized 22nd (month not stated). Sponsors, Joseph and Mary Ann Grünewald.

Original book, page 32.

Mcquys, [McHugh?] Catharine, of John and Mary Mcquys, born January 9, 1803, baptized May 6th. Sponsors, Martin and Elizabeth O'Bryen [Obrien?].

Wheit, [White?] David, of Anthony and Mary Wheit, three years old, baptized May 12th. Sponsors, Michael and Elizabeth Calagher [Gallagher?].

Clerick, Daniel, of —— and Helena Clerick, born July 9th (evidently of the preceding year), baptized May 12th. Sponsors, Henry Manteck [Montague?] and Mary Mcqueyer [McGuire?].

Dagourthy, [Dougherty?] Margaret, of James and Elizabeth Dagour-

33

thy, born March 1st, baptized May 12th. Sponsors, Manasses and Catharine Dagourthy.

Dagourthy, Daniel, of Manasses and Catharine Dagourthy, born May 4th, baptized May 12th. Sponsors, Jacob Broun [Brown?] and Henna (probably Hanna) Calagher [Gallagher ?].

Tygard [Taggart?] John, of Abraham and Anna Tygard, born November 31st (probably of the preceding year), baptized May 12th. Sponsors, Henry MeCkan [McCann ?] and Rose Algoyer [Allgeier?].

Broun, [Brown?] Francisca, of Jacob and Francisca Broun, born January 5th, baptized May 16th. Sponsors, James Calleghar [Gallagher?] and Bridget Dagouthy [Dougherty?].

Mequeyer [McGuire?] Anna, of Patrick and Anna Mcqueyer, born June 20th (evidently of the preceding year), baptized May 20th. Sponsors, John and Margaret Dogourthy.

Archsman [Assmann? or Ashman?] William, of William and Mary Archsman, born August 9th, baptized May 20th. Sponsors, Patrick and Bridget McDemord [McDermott?].

Meglochly, [McLaughlin?] Genevieve, of Thomas and Genevieve Meglochly, born September 20th (evidently of the preceding year), baptized May 20th. Sponsors, Daniel and Margaret Thimory.

Thymori, Mary, of Dionysius and Mary Thymori, born December 11th (evidently of the preceding year), baptized May 20th. Sponsors, Patrick Michen [Meehan?] and Anna Kely [Kelly?].

Clerick, Elizabeth, of Jacob and Catharine Clerick, born December 11th (evidently of the preceding year), baptized May 20th. Sponsors, John and Mary Kuhn.

Crecck [Craig?], Prudentia, of Joseph and Ann Creeck, born January 2d, baptized May 20th. Sponsors, Juy (Hugh ?) and Prudentia Boyl.

Creck [Craig?], Nicholas, of Joseph and Anna Creck, born July 22, 1801, baptized May 26th. Sponsors, Elisaius and Mary Therby [Durby?].

Meccferry, Edward, of Neal and Anna Meccferry, born March 15, 1801, baptized May 26th. Sponsors, Joseph and Catharine Meccferry.

Rogers, Amelia, of Frank and Elizabeth Rogers, born April 1st, baptized May 26th. Sponsors, Jacob Broun [Brown?] and Mary Aelentayer.

Original book, page 33.

Zinsdorf, Henry, of George and Anna Mary Zinsdorf, born April 12th, baptized May 31st. Sponsors, Dionysius and Catharine Handel.

Blayton, Frances, a woman received into the Church. Baptized May 27th.

Noell, Isaias, of Peter and Margaret Noell, November 10th (without stating what happened on that day), previously of no religion, baptized June 3rd. Sponsors, John and Martha Magoy [McCoy?].

34

Ellesen [Ellison ?] Elizabeth, of John and Mary Ellesen, born September 6th, 1803, baptized June 10th. Sponsors, Timothy Conner and Catharine Broun.

Mechyn [Maginn, McKean ?] Joseph, of Berny and Salome Mechyn, born October 22nd, 1803, baptized June 10th, Sponsors, Dionysius Brogen and Mary Broun.

Kelly, James, of John and Martha Kelly, two years old, baptized June 24th. Sponsors, Peter and Catharine Roger.

Noell, Mary, of Joseph and Margaret Noell, born March 5th, baptized July 1st. Sponsors, Simon Ruffner and Margaret Griffy.

Roger, Hugo, of Anthony and Rose Roger, born June 3rd, baptized July 1st. Sponsors, John Macher [Maher ?] and Bridget Schorthy.

Original book, page 34.

Septer, Elizabeth, of Frederick and Anna Maria Septer, born April 23rd, baptized July 8th. Sponsors, Joseph, and Margaret Noell.

—— Peter Joseph, born June 27th, baptized July 9th. Sponsors, Peter Clearfield and Mary Carriens [Cairns or Kerens ?].

O'Dannel [O'Donnell ?] Catharine, of Daniel and Cecilia O'Dannel, born October 2nd, baptized October 28th. Sponsors, Carol and Bridget Roger.

Kaess, Peter, of Joséph and Mary Kaess, born October 9th, baptized November 1st. Sponsors, Henry and Elizabeth Brick.

Original book, page 35.

Bayl [Boyle ?] John, of Felix and Elizabeth Bayl (date of birth not given), baptized November 18th. Sponsors, Dionysius Delery and his wife.

Victor, David, of John and Mary Victor, born October 1st, baptized November 19th. Sponsors, David Victor and Elizabeth, a widow.

Mecferry, Daniel, of Timothy and Susan Mecferry, born August 9, baptized November 24th. Sponsors, Michael Mequy [McHugh?] and Mary Dugen [Dugan ?].

Carr, Theresa, of Patrick and Petronilla Carr, born October 15, baptized November 24th. Sponsors, Charles and Genevieve Mecferien.

Carr, James, of Manasses and Catharine Carr, born July 18th, baptized November 24th. Sponsors, James Carr and Bridget Boyl.

Dugen [Dugan ?] Salome, of Daniel and Catharine Dugen, born October 25th, baptized November 24th. Sponsors, Neal Meccbraid [McBride ?] and Helen Carr.

Lemain [Lehman or Leamen ?] Stephen, of Lawrence and Elizabeth Lemain, born May 10th, baptized November 24th. Sponsors, James and Mary Carr.

1805

Brick, Mary, of Peter and Margaret Brick, born December 9th (evidently of the preceding year), baptized February 24th. Sponsors, Matthias and Mary Brick.

35

Daguorthy [Dougherty?] (name of child not given), of Charles and Anna Daguorthy, born November 13 (evidently of preceding year), baptized March 24. Sponsors, James Meguy [McHugh?] and Susan, his mother.

Isly [Easly?], Sara, of Andrew and Elizabeth Isly, born May 20th, baptized April 14th. Sponsors, Henry and Margaret Kuhn.

Original book, page 36.

Merckell [Markle?], Jacob, of John and Barbara Merckell, born March 3, baptized April 14. Sponsors, Martin and Magdalen Müller.

Septer, John, of Adam and Mary Septer, born July 28th, baptized April 14th. Sponsors, Patrick and Margaret Gryffen [Griffin?].

Dougerthy [Dougherty?], Mary, of Patrick and Sara Dougerthy, born October 10th (evidently of the preceding year), baptized April 14th. Sponsors, John and Helen Dougerthy.

Meglafferty, James, of John and Mary Meglafferty, born December 10th, baptized May 23rd. Sponsors, Patrick Ferry and Bridget Roger.

Mcdavid [McDevitt?], Elizabeth, of Henry and Elizabeth Mcdavid, born August 8th (evidently of the preceding year), baptized June 2nd. Sponsors, William and Catharine O'Hara.

Branner, Mary, of James and Salome Branner, born September 12 (evidently of the preceding year), baptized June 2nd. Sponsors, Patrick and Catharine Levy.

Scholl, Henry, of John and Mary Scholl, born March 18th, baptized June 2nd. Sponsors, James Mecfoll [McFaul?] and Susan Queen [Quinn?].

Müller, John, of Jacob and Sara Müller, born March 20th, baptized June 2nd. Sponsors, Neal Meclarsy and Johana Lauchely.

Doffy [Duffy], Frank, of Patrick and Martha Doffy, born December 2nd (evidently of the preceding year), baptized June 2nd. Sponsors, Peter Declary and Bridget Mecbraid [McBride?].

Denny, Salome, of Dionysius and Julia Denny, born March 1st, baptized June 2nd. Sponsors, Anthony and Catharine Keller.

Brannen, Susan, of John and Anna Brannen, born February 2, baptized June 2. Sponsors, Edward and Eva Meccferren.

Reyly [Reilly?], Elizabeth, of Martin and Anna Reyly, born February 11th, baptized June 2nd. Sponsors, Darby and Mary his wife.

Dagourthy, Anna, of Charles and Anna Dagourthy, born March 3rd, baptized June 2nd. Sponsors, Dionysius Morfy [Murphy?] and Mary Kelly.

Mechafly, Anna, of ——— and Eleanor Mechafly, born February 1st, baptized June 2. (No sponsors are given.)

Original book, page 37.

Branner, Mary, of Michael and Mary Branner, born April 15, baptized June 2d. Sponsors, Christopher and Catharine Branner.

Good, Nicholas, of Balthasar and Rose Good, five years old, baptized June 5th. Sponsors, Stephen and Catharine Branner.

—— (evidently Good), Susan, of Balthasar and Rose, three years old, on the 12th of May. Baptized June 5th. Sponsor, Rose Meccfolh [McFaul?].

Good, Rose, of Balthasar and Rose Good, born December 23d, 1804, baptized June 5th. Sponsors, Julius Meccanigen and wife.

Massercop, Margaret, of —— and Anna Massercop, born in 1803, baptized June 5th. Sponsors, Jacob May and Anna Meckennegy.

Greven, John George, of John and Margaret Greven, two years old, baptized June 5th. Sponsors, Joseph and Eleanor Kitsly.

Gyllen, [Gillen?], James Henry, of Philip and Rose Gyllen, born May 5th, baptized June 5th. Sponsors, George Mecanigen and Mary Gyllen.

Schmolder, Mary Anne, of Edward and Catharine Schmolder, born May 4th, baptized June 5th. Sponsors, James and Genevieve Meccfolh [McFaul?].

Gibsen [Gibson?] Margaret, of William and Margaret Gibsen, born February 3, baptized June 5th. Sponsors, Julius and Petronilla Meccanigen.

Massercop, Anna, of —— and Anna Massercop, five years old, baptized June 5th. Sponsors, Mary Morfy [Murphy?] and Patrick Brannen.

Greven, Christina, of George and Margaret Greven, (date of birth not given), baptized June 5th. Sponsors, David and Anna Michen [Meehan?].

Clerick, Rose, of John and Helen Clerick, born April 17th, baptized June 9th. Sponsors, Felix Daniel and Rose Mequaeyer [McGuire?].

Original book, page 38.

Daniel, Mary, of Felix and Charity Daniel, born April 12th, baptized June 9th. Sponsors, John and Eleanor McQuayer [McGuire].

Bready, [Brady?] Thomas, of Lawrence and Catharine Bready, eight years old, baptized June 9th. Sponsors, John Cannedy and Anna Doffyn.

Bready, [Brady?], Bernard, of Lawrence and Catherine Bready, five years old, baptized June 9th. Sponsors, John Spedy and Elizabeth Stoner.

Dagourthy [Dougherty?], Mary, of Roger and Eleanor Dagourthy, born July 2d, baptized June 9th. Sponsors, Jacob Braun and Elizabeth Dagourthy.

Weith [White], Anna, of Anthony and Mary Weith, born February 10th, baptized June 10th. Sponsors, Michael Galagar [Gallagher?] and Elizabeth Weith.

Laden, Genevieve, of James and Anna Laden, born May 16th, baptized June 15th. Sponsors, Patrick and Bridget Mecchiffisen.

37

Mony, Jacob, of William and Mary Mony, born December 24th, baptized June 15th. Sponsors, Jacob Laden and Anna Ferry.

Callenz, [Collins?], Isaac, of Daniel and Catharine Callenz, four years old, baptized June 15th. Sponsors, William Mony and Catharine Dagourthy.

Callenz [Collins?], John, of John and Catharine Callenz, three years old, baptized June 15th. Sponsors, Jeremiah and Margaret Liffing.

Workman, Henrietta, of Jacob and Mary Workman, born February 18th, baptized June 15th. Sponsors, Nicholas and Theme Gelaspy [Gillespie?].

Wambold, Margaret, of Luke and Margaret Wambold, born February 12th, baptized June 15th. Sponsors, Edward Borns [Burns?] and Anne Trucks.

Michen [Meehan?], James, of William and Elizabeth Michen, born on the 2d (month not given), baptized June 15th. Sponsors, Daniel and Margaret Commery.

Original book, page 39.

Cinnen [Keenan?] Margaret and Mary Anne, William and Elizabeth, brothers and sisters, born of Jeremiah and Margaret Cinnen. Sponsors, Thomas Meclachlen [McLaughlin?] and wife.

Gelaspy [Gillespie?], Elizabeth, of Nicholas Gelaspy Jr. and his wife, born April 7th, baptized June 15th. Sponsors, George Trucks and Mary Worckman.

Gelaspy [Gillespie?], Julia, of James and Anna Gelaspy, born November 1st (evidently of the preceding year), baptized June 15th. Sponsors, —— Mecchery [McSherry?] and Ann Gelaspy.

Levain, Thomas, of Timothy and Mary Levain, seven years old, baptized June 15th. Sponsor, Denis O'Breyen [O'Brien?]

Mcelrayer [McElroy?] Margaret, of John and Margaret Mcelrayer, born November 11th (evidently of the preceding year), baptized June 16th. Sponsors, William Migen [Meehan?] and Anna Meckiffisin.

Figter [Fechter or Feichter?] Genevieve, of David and Genevieve Figter, six years old, baptized June 16th. Sponsors, John and Elizabeth Figter.

Gery [Gary?], Elizabeth, of Felix and Anna Gery, born November 15th (evidently of the preceding year), baptized June 17th. Sponsors, Michael Dorren and Anna Drucks.

Gery [Gary?], Cassidorus, of Felix and Anna Gery, two years old, baptized June 17th. Sponsors, Nicholas and Theme Gelaspy [Gillespie?].

Bellsaind, Sara, aged twenty-seven years, and married: previously of no religion, baptized June 22, and at once admitted into the Church.

Dorbain [Durbin?], William, of Nicholas and Catharine Dorbain, born November 27th (evidently of the preceding year), baptized June 22nd. Sponsors, Lawrence Dorbain and Clara Hardin.

38

Carr, Anna, of Charles and Anna Carr, born November 27th (evidently of the preceding year), baptized June 22nd. Sponsors, James and Catharine Meckingly [McKinley ?].

Meccferly, Charles, of Manasses and Catharine Meccferly, born May 15th, baptized June 22nd. Sponsors, Daniel and Genevieve Boyl.

Original book, page 40.

Galeger [Gallagher ?], James, of Anthony and Bridget Galeger, born March 19th, baptized June 22nd. Sponsors, Daniel and Susan Boyl Harden.

Meccbraid [McBride ?], Margaret, of Nicholas Meccbraid and his wife, born April 30th, baptized June 22nd. Sponsors, Patrick Boyl and Margaret Meccguy [McHugh ?].

Meccguy [McHugh ?] Catharine, of Michael and Petronilla Meccguy, born June 19th, baptized June 22nd. Sponsors, Manasses and Catharine Car [Carr ?].

Müller, Joseph, of Martin and Magdalen Müller, born June 22nd, baptized August 11th. Sponsors, John Henrich and Magdalen Kuhn.

Brick, Theresa, of Henry Brick (name of the mother omitted), born July 12th, baptized August 15th. Sponsors, Henry Kuhn and Elizabeth Brick.

Ruffner John Jacob, of Simon and Mary Barbara Ruffner, born July 9th, baptized August 15th. Sponsors, Jacob Kuhn and Catharine Seyverth [Seybert ?], maiden.

Griffy [Greavy ?], Rachel, of Henry and Magdalen Griffy, born June 22nd, baptized August 17th. Sponsors, Patrick and Margaret Griffy.

Kely [Kelly ?], James Henry, of Patrick and Margaret Kely, born January 19th, baptized August 25th. Sponsors, Henry Kuhn and Elizabeth Brick, maiden.

Meclosscy [McCloskey ?], Daniel, of John and Rose Meclosscy, born March 8th, baptized September 8th. Sponsors, Jacob and Catharine Kuyn [Kuhn ?].

Meclosscy [McCloskey?], Petronilla, of John and Rose Meclosscy, born January 15, baptized September 8th. Sponsors, Joseph and Catharine Schmidt.

Meclosscy [McCloskey?] John, of John and Rose Meclosscy, born March 1st, baptized September 8th. Sponsors, Patrick Mecay [McKay?], and Catharine Ruffner.

, Note: The years of birth of the children of the preceding entries have been omitted. The children evidently are brothers and sisters, and must have been born in different years.

Roger, Michael, of Michael and Elizabeth Roger, born April 18, baptized September 8th. Sponsors, Patrick Dougerthy [Dougherty?], and Mary Seiffert [Seybert?].

39

Original book, page 41.

Mecloscy [McCloskey?] James, of John Meclosscy (name of mother omitted), born March 27th, baptized September 8th. Sponsors, Michael and Catharine Hagey.

Meclosscy [McCloskey?], Michael, of Nicholas Meclosscy (name of mother omitted], born March 11th, baptized September 8th. Sponsors, Mecelvay [McKelvey?] and Margaret.

Coller, Mary, of Michael and Magdalen Coller, born October 5th (evidently of the preceding year), baptized September 15th. Sponsors, Frederick and Mary Septer.

Ruffner, Simon, of George and Elizabeth Ruffner, born on the 7th of this month, baptized September 22nd. Sponsors, Simon and Catharine Ruffner.

September at Bofflo.

Archibleck, Mary, of —— Archibleck and Mary, his wife. Date of birth not given, baptized September 28th. Sponsors, Daniel and Mary Meguy [McGee?].

Keyl [Kyle?] Elizabeth, of John and Elizabeth Keyl, date of birth not given, baptized September 28th. Sponsors, John and Elizabeth Archibleck.

Pock, Susan, of William and Anna Pock, date of birth not given, baptized September 28th. Sponsors, Bernard and Catharine Hagen.

Hegen [Hagen?] Anna, of Bernard and Catharine Hagen, date of birth not given, baptized September 28th. Sponsors, William and Mary Anne Schiltz [Schultz?].

Michen [Meehan?], James, of John and Mary Michen, date of birth not given, baptized September 28th. Sponsors, Thomas and Elizabeth Dugen [Dugan?].

Hergy [Hershey?], Thomas, of Robert and Elizabeth Hergy, date of birth not given, baptized September 28th. Sponsors, John and Mary Michen [Meehan?].

Gelaspy [Gillespie?] Anna, of Hughy and Anna Gelaspy, date of birth not given, baptized September 28th. Sponsors, Connel and Mary O'Dannel.

Clugency, Margaret, of John and Mary Clugency, date of birth not given, baptized September 28th. Sponsors, John Caligher [Gallagher?] and Mary Mecbraid [McBride?].

Dugen [Dugan?] Catharine, of Michael and Bridget Dugen, date of birth not given, baptized September 28th. Sponsors, Peter Dugen and Elizabeth Heister.

Dugen, James, of Neal and Anna Dugen, date of birth not given, baptized September 28th. Sponsors, Robert and Elizabeth Hergen.

Original book, page 42.

Dagerthy [Dougherty?] Patrick, of Neal and Crescentia Dagerthy, date of birth not given, baptized September 28th. Sponsors, James Ferry and Mary Dagerthy.

Meckeley, Daniel, of John and Susan Meckeley, date of birth not given, baptized September 28th. Sponsors, Patrick and Mary O'Dannel.

Duffy, Margaret, of Charles and Petronilla Duffy, date of birth not given, baptized September 18th (apparently a mistake for the 28th). Sponsors, Michael and Margaret Dugen.

O'Dannel [O'Donnell ?], Bridget, of Connel and Mary O'Dannel, date of birth not given, baptized September 28th. Sponsors, Dionysius O'Dannel and Sara Hartman.

Gelaspy [Gillespie ?], John, of John and Elizabeth Gelaspy, date of birth not given, baptized September 28th. Sponsors, John and Barbara Duffing.

Dagerthy [Dougherty ?], Hughy, of James and Anna Dagerthy, date of birth not given, baptized September 28th. Sponsors, John and Elizabeth Gelaspy [Gillespie ?].

Roger, Thomas, of Connel and Anna Roger, date of birth not given, baptized September 28th. Sponsors, Patrick and Mary Meckellrey [McElroy ?]

Schweny [Sweeney,], Hughy, of Charles and Mary Schweny, date of birth not given, baptized September 30th. Sponsors, John and Anna Duffy.

Hartman, Margaret, of Philip and Margaret Hartman, date of birth not given, baptized September 30th. Sponsors, William and Mary Duffy.

Anderson, Joseph, of Joseph and Mary Anderson, date of birth not given, baptized September 30th. Sponsors, James Meclachlen [McLaughlin ?], and Catharine Schweny [Sweeney ?].

Schweny [Sweeny?], James, of John and Bridget Schweny, date of birth not given, baptized September 30th. Sponsors, John and Catharine Hagen.

Hagen, Bridget, of John and Bridget Hagen, date of birth not given, baptized September 30th. Sponsors, John and Bridget Schweny [Sweeney?].

Hagen, Margaret, of John and Catharine Hagen, date of birth not given, baptized September 30th. Sponsors, John and Bridget Schweny [Sweeney?].

Hagen, John, of John and Catharine Hagen, date of birth not given, baptized September 30th. Sponsors, John and Bridget Schweny [Sweeney?].

Schweny [Sweeney?] Solomon, of John and Bridget Schweny, date of birth not given, baptized September 30th. Sponsors, Neal and Mary Mecbraid [McBride].

Original book, page 43.

Meguy [McHugh?] John, of Patrick and Bridget Meguy, date of birth not given, baptized September 26th. Sponsors, Francis and Elizabeth Meguy.

Isly [Easly?] William, of Caspar and Elizabeth Isly, date of birth not given, baptized September 26th. Sponsors, William and Mary Schiltz [Schultz?].

Meguy [McHugh?] Charles, of Daniel and Bridget Meguy, date of birth not given, baptized September 26th. Sponsors, Caspar and Elizabeth Isly [Easly?].

Meguy [McHugh?], Bernard, of Daniel and Bridget Meguy, date of birth not given, baptized September 26th. Sponsors, Patrick and Bridget Meguy.

Meguy [McHugh,], Peter, of Charles and Anna Meguy, date of birth not given, baptized September 26th. Sponsors, Patrick and Bridget Meguy.

Meguichen [McGuigan], Daniel, of John and Cecilia Meguichen, date of birth not given, baptized September 28th. Sponsors, Michael and Petronilla Meguy [McHugh?].

Megrafferty [McCafferty?], Genevieve, of Charles and Salome Megrafferty, date of birth not given, baptized September 28th. Sponsors, Balthasar and Mary Thompson.

Mecbraid [McBride?], Stephen, of Patrick and Mary Mecbraid, date of birth not given, baptized September 28th. Sponsors, Anthony and Catharine Kelly.

Callegar [Gallagher?], James, of ――― and Anna Callegar, date of birth not given, baptized September 28th. Sponsors, Patrick and Mary Mecbraid [McBride?].

Callegar, Hughy, of Hughy and Genevieve Callegar, date of birth not given, baptized September 28th. Sponsors, Peter and Petronilla Callegar.

Hagerthy [Hagerty?], Robert, of Thomas and Anna Hagerthy, date of birth not given, baptized September 28th. Sponsors, Edward and Cecilia Schweny [Sweeney?].

Schweny [Sweeney?], John, of Edward and Sara Schweny, date of birth not given, baptized September 28th. Sponsors, Richard and Anna Meguy [McHugh?].

Whey, Anna, of Patrick and Petronilla Whey, date of birth not given, baptized September 28th. Sponsors, John and Anna Mecbraid [McBride?].

Doffy [Duffy?], John, of John and Anna Doffy, date of birth not given, baptized September 28th. Sponsors, Frank and Anna Duffy.

Original book, page 44.

Forcker [Foraker?], William, of John and Rose Forcker, date of birth not given, baptized September 28th. Sponsors, John and Anna Keyl [Kyle?].

Schweny [Sweeney], Bridget, of Michael and Anna Schweny, date of birth not given, baptized September 28th. Sponsors, Andrew and Susan Dugen [Dugan?].

Daiman [Diamond?], Joseph, a son of John Daiman, Jacob, a brother and William, a relative of the same father, baptized October 7th. Sponsors, Edward and Susan Kohl.

Gery [Gary?], Margaret, of Michael and Mary Gery, date of birth not given, baptized October 7th. Sponsors, Peter and Margaret Dreschler.

Braiden, Charles, of Jacob and Helen Braiden, date of birth not given, baptized October 7th. Sponsor, Peter Thiden.

Moholland [Mulholland?], Daniel, of Daniel and Helen Moholland, date of birth not given, baptized October 7th. No sponsors given.

Higens [Higgins?], James, of Andrew and Margaret Higens, date of birth not given, baptized October 7th. Sponsors, Manasses and Frances Brodlyn.

Green, James, of James and Frances Green, date of birth not given, baptized October 7th. Sponsors, Gabriel and Margaret Mecnackel.

Mecbraid [McBride?], Neal, of Patrick and Mary Mecbraid, date of birth not given, baptized October 16th. Sponsors, Anna Door and Mary Cinckley.

Note: The names of two females are here clearly given as sponsors.

Meckeny [McKenna?], Bartholomew, of ―― and Margaret Meckeny, date of birth not given, baptized October 16th. Sponsors, Cornelius Mecbraid [McBride?] and Salome Schweny [Sweeney?].

Schweny [Sweeney?], Morgan, of Alexander and Salome Schweny, date of birth not given, baptized October 16th. Sponsors, James and Mary Mecbraid [McBride?].

Mecbraid [McBride?], Patrick, of Patrick and Mary Mecbraid, date of birth not given, baptized October 16th. Sponsors, Michael and Margaret Denny.

Mecbraid [McBride?], Cornelius, of Edward and Catharine Mecbraid, date of birth not given, baptized October 16th. Sponsors, Patrick and Mary Mecbraid [McBride?].

Meguy [McHugh?], Anna, of ―― and Anna Meguy, date of birth not given, baptized October 16th. Sponsors, Bartholomew and Bridget Mecbraid [McBride?].

Carl [Carroll?], Charles, of Hughy and Anna Carl, date of birth not given, baptized October 16th. Sponsors, Bartholomew and Bridget Mecbraid [McBride?].

Original book, page 45.

Carole [Carroll?], James, of Hughy and Anna Carole, date of birth not given, baptized October 16th. Sponsors, Bartholomew and Bridget Mecbraid [McBride?].

Grünewald, Mary Elizabeth, of Joseph and Mary Grünewald, date of birth not given, baptized October 2nd. Sponsors, Nicholas and Mary Walhy.

Seyffert [Seybert?], Matthias, of Matthias and Elizabeth Seyffert, date of birth not given, baptized October 2nd. Sponsors, Huighy and Genevieve Callegar.

Cembor [Kemper?], Anthony, of John and Barbara Cembor, date of birth not given, baptized October 2nd. Sponsors, Matthias and Elizabeth Seyffert.

O'Donnel, Mary, of Connel and Bridget O'Donnel, date of birth not given, baptized October 2nd. Sponsors, John Welsch and Rose Dugen [Dugan?].

Mecafferty [McCafferty?], Salome, of Neal and Mary Mecafferty, date of birth not given, baptized October 2nd. Sponsors, Connel and Anna Roger.

Daiman [Diamond?], Daniel, of John and Petronilla Daiman, date of birth not given, baptized October 6th. Sponsors, Philip and Elizabeth Meguy [McHugh?].

Daiman [Diamond?], Petronilla, of John and Eleanor Daiman, date of birth not given, baptized October 6th. Sponsors, Edward Mecfferrien and Petronilla Scharty.

Schorty, Anna, of Anthony and Bridget Schorty, date of birth not given, baptized October 6th. Sponsors, William and Genevieve Glancy.

Brothly, Anna, of Manasses and Anna Brothly, date of birth not given, baptized October 6th. Sponsors, Joseph Mollen [Mullen?] and Mary Meckenhady.

Daiman [Diamond?], Philip, of John and Petronilla Daiman date of birth not given, baptized October 6th. Sponsors, Edward and Susan Hohn [Huhn?].

Roger, Catharine, of John and Cecilia Roger, date of birth not given, baptized October 6th. Sponsors, Daniel and Mary Reed.

Lukoy, Elizabeth, of Joseph and Mary Lukoy, date of birth not given, baptized October 6th. Sponsors, Jacob and Anna Denny.

Original book, page 46.

Schmidt, Susan, of John and Margaret Schmidt, date of birth not given, baptized October 6th. Sponsors, Christopher and Margaret Gloss [Glass?].

Kiell, John, of John and Sara Kiell, date of birth not given, baptized October 6th. Sponsors, John and Margaret Schmidt.

Isaac, Elizabeth, of John and Mary Isaac, date of birth not given, baptized October 6th. Sponsors, Edward and Anna Fiell.

Meckenalldy [McNulty?], James, of James and Mary Meckenalldy, date of birth not given, baptized October 6th. Sponsors, Jacob and Anna Reyhen [Ryan?].

Lin [Lynn?], Margaret, of James and Elizabeth Lin, date of birth not given, baptized October 6th. Sponsors, Hughy and Catharine Morgen.

Schwiny [Sweeney?], James, of John and Bridget Schwiny, date of birth not given, baptized October 6th. Sponsors, John and Catharine Hagin.

Hagen, Bridget, of John and Bridget Hagen, date of birth not given, baptized October 6th. Sponsors, John and Catharine Hagen.

Hagen, Margaret, of John and Catharine Hagen, date of birth not given, baptized October 6th. Sponsors, John and Bridget Schweny [Sweeney?].

Hagen, John, of John and Catharine Hagen, date of birth not given, baptized October 6th. Sponsors, John and Bridget Schweny [Sweeney?].

Schweny [Sweeney?], Salome, and Anna, of John and Bridget Schweny, date of birth not given, baptized October 6th. Sponsors, Neal and Mary Mecbraid [McBride?].

Tenny [Taney?], Nicholas, of Meils and Margaret Tenny, date of birth not given, baptized October 6th. Sponsors, Patrick and Mary Mecbraid [McBride?].

Tenny [Taney?], Susan, of Meils and Margaret Tenny, date of birth not given, baptized October 6th. Sponsors, Cornelius Mecbraid [McBride?] and Bridget Schweny [Sweeney?].

MecLachelen [McLaughlin?], Thomas, of Henry and Anna Meclachelen, and Anna, a sister, and William and Henry, brothers, children of —— and Anna Meclachlen, baptized October 6th. Sponsors, John Meclachlen and Henry his brother with their wives.

Original book, page 47.

Morfy [Murphy?], James, of Dionysius and Elizabeth Morfy, date of birth not given, baptized November 3rd. Sponsors, Jacob and Anna May.

Therren, Charles, of Patrick and Margaret Therren, date of birth not given, baptized November 3rd. Sponsors, James and Susan Queen [Quinn?].

Clenegal, Helen, of Huighy and Mary Clenegal, date of birth not given, baptized November 3rd. Sponsors, John Meccfoull [McFaul?] and Anne his sister.

Cannery, Thomas and Margaret, of Thomas and Margaret Cannery, date of birth not given, baptized November 7th. Sponsors, —— Meckelly and Honora Cannery.

Cannery, Genevieve, of Thomas and Margaret Cannery, date of birth not given, baptized November 7th. Sponsors, John and Martha Kelly.

Kelly, Catharine, of Thomas and Margaret Kelly, date of birth not given, baptized November 7th. Sponsors, Thomas and Margaret Cannery.

Arnst, Elizabeth, of Jacob and Margaret Arnst, date of birth not given, baptized November 23rd. Sponsors Henry Brick and Elizabeth Reinzel.

Ditter, Henry, of Henry and Catharine Ditter, a year old, baptized December 5th. Sponsors, Henry Kuhn and Elizabeth Müller.

FATHER PETER HELBRON'S GREENSBURG, PA., REGISTER

Copied from the original by the Rev. Father John, O. S. B., of Saint Vincent's Abbey, Pennsylvania. Translated by Lawrence F. Flick, M.D., LL.D.

1806

Handel, Joseph, of Dionysius and Catharine Handel, six weeks old, baptized January 5th. Sponsors, Joseph Handel and Mary Braun [Brown?].

Mcfeyn, William, of Patrick and Anna Mcfeyn, born July 31st (evidently of the preceding year), baptized March 9th. Sponsors, Dionysius Conner and Elizabeth, his sister.

Original book, page 48.

Vagener, Henry, of John and Barbara Vagener, born February 25th, baptized April 3d. Sponsors Henry and Elizabeth Brik.

Septer, Margaret, of Adam and Mary Septer, born January 14th, baptized April 6th. Sponsors, Peter and Margaret Noell.

Ruffner, Salome, of Christian and Mary Ruffner, born January 4th, baptized April 6th. Sponsors, John Henry Ruffner and Mary Ruffner, maiden.

Duff, Anna, of Paul and Anna Duff, born January 8th, baptized April 6th. Sponsors, John Hargen and Bridget Rogers.

Brannen, Peter, of Michael and Mary Brannen, born April 2d, baptized May 4th. Sponsors, Anthony Bern [Byrne?] and his wife.

Schmidt, Catharine, of Matthias and Elizabeth Schmidt, born January 1st, baptized May 4th. Sponsors, Nicholas and Susan Schwoerer.

Reily, Margaret, of Martin and Anna Reily, date of birth not given, baptized May 4th. Sponsors, Patrick Hely [Healy?] and Anna, his wife.

Reily, Mary, of Martin and Anna Reily, three years old, baptized May 4th. Sponsors, one of the Hely family and Anna.

Lachly, Salome, of John anad Margaret Lachly, born April 5th, baptized May 4th. Sponsors, Andrew Claudwill and his wife.

Gihlen, Margaret, of Philip and Susan Gihlen, born April 9th, baptized May 5th. Sponsors, Andrew Gihlen and Mary Gihlen, widow.

Mecdonnel [McDonald?], Rose, of ——— Mecdonnel and Rose, his wife, born June 30th (evidently of the preceding year), baptized May 10th. Sponsors, John and Catharine Meyer.

Wite [White?], Anthony, of James and Elizabeth Wite, date of birth not given, baptized May 11th. Sponsors, —— Quickly [Quigly?] and wife.

Galeghar [Gallagher?], Charles, of Michael and Margaret Galeghar, date of birth not given, baptized May 11th. Sponsors not given.

——, Jacob, six years old (surname of child not given and names of parents not given), baptized May 11th. Sponsors, —— Schoerer and Mary Haegen.

Original book, page 49.

White, James, of —— White and Elizabeth, his wife, date of birth not given, baptized May 11th. Sponsors, James and Cecilia Reily.

Haege, George, of Abraham and Anna Haege, born October 4th (evidently of the preceding year), baptized May 11th. Sponsors, John and Anna McQuire [McGuire?].

Reily, Anna, of James and Cecilia Reily, date of birth not given, baptized May 11th. Sponsors, John Meguire [McGuire?] and Rose Manteck [Montague?].

Galegher [Gallagher?], Margaret of Michael and Margaret Galegher, date of birth not given, baptized May 11th. Sponsors, James Braun [Brown?] and his sister.

Wilterstaedt, Rose, of John and Petronilla Wilterstaedt, date of birth not given, baptized May 11th. Sponsors, Clearsen and Margaret.

Daugerthy [Dougherty?], Charles, of James and Anna Daugerthy, date of birth not given, baptized May 12th. Sponsors, John Quickly and Bridget Daugerthy.

Roger, Anna, of Frank and Elizabeth Roger, date of birth not given, baptized May 11th. Sponsors, Simon Manteck [Montague?] and Mary McQuier [McGuire?].

Victor, Anna, of John and Margaret Victor, date of birth not given, baptized May 18th. Sponsors, Michael and Elizabeth Schoerer.

Thern, Mails Joseph, of Michael Thern and his wife Elizabeth, born July 19th (evidently of the preceding year), baptized May 18th. Sponsors, Edward Borns [Burns?] and Anna Trox.

Galeghar [Gallagher?], Susan, of Adam and Mary Galeghar, born March 2d, baptized May 19th. Sponsors, Charles and Catharine Haergen.

Morris, Margaret, of John and Catharine Morris, three years old, baptized May 19th. Sponsors, Patrick Mecguier [McGuire?] and Eva Victor.

Morris, Reuben, of John and Catharine Morris, six years old, baptized May 19th. Sponsors, Gerard Meccherry [McSherry?] and Bridget Mecdemart [McDermott?].

Deleny, Elizabeth, of Dionysius and Mary Deleny, date of birth not given, baptized May 19th. Sponsors, Martin and Mary Therren.

47

Meccherry [McSherry?], Margaret, of Gerhard and Catharine Meccherry, born July 15th (evidently of the preceding year), baptized
May 19th. Sponsors, George and Mary Trox.

Victor, Mary, of John and Mary Victor, born March 25th, baptized
May 25th. Sponsors, Hughy Beyl [Boyle?] and Mary Casthler.

Phillippi, Thomas, of Thomas and Mary Phillippi, date of birth not
given, baptized May 25th. Sponsors, Jacob Eysenaagel and Susan
Bayl [Boyle?].

Gerry, James, of Timothy and Susan Gerry, date of birth not given,
baptized May 25th. Sponsors, Patrick Car [Carr?] and Sophie
Mecferryn.

Mecbraid [McBride?], Petronilla, of ——— Mecbraid and Catharine
his wife, date of birth not given, baptized May 25th. Sponsors,
John and Mary Meckiver.

Caleghar [Gallagher?], Catharine, of John and Mary Caleghar, date of
birth not given, baptized May 25th. Sponsors, Hughy Bail [Boyle?]
and Catharine Galeghar.

Isly [Easly?], Margaret, of Ferdinand and Margaret Isly, born June
8th, baptized June 9th. Sponsors, John Borgoon [Burgoon?] and
Mary Müller.

Carren, Salome, of John and Margaret Carren, born April 17th, baptized June 22d. Sponsors, James Roger and Eppy Coll.

Bivers, Barbara, of Thomas and Elizabeth Bivers, born March 2d, baptized June 29th. Sponsors, John Henry and Mary Zinsdorff.

Bivers, Elizabeth, of Thomas and Elizabeth Bivers, two years old, baptized June 22d. Sponsor, Elizabeth Henling.

Ruffner, Mary Magdalen, of George and Sibylla Ruffner, born May
13th, baptized July 13th. Sponsors, Simon Noel and Catharine Isly
[Easly?].

Meccefferty [McCafferty?], Charles, of Jacob Meccefferty and Catharine his wife, born May 23d, baptized July 20th. Sponsors, John
and Mary Chalegar [Gallagher?].

Schilz [Schulz?], Catharine, of William and Mary Schilz, born March
27th, baptized July 28th. Sponsors, Simon and Catharine Ruffner.

Noel, Joseph, of Joseph and Margaret Noel, born August 3d, baptized
October 5th. Sponsors, Joseph Schmidt and Elizabeth, maiden.

1807

Merckell, George, of John and Barbara Merckell, born November 13th
(evidently of the preceding year), baptized March 29th. Sponsors,
John Henry and Mary Zinsdorff, maiden.

Brick, Theresa, of Peter and Margaret Brick, born January 21st, baptized March 29th. Sponsors, George Ruffner and Theresa Brick, maiden.

Müller, Mary, of Martin and Magdalen Müller, born December 25th (evidently of the preceding year), baptized March 29th. Sponsors, Frederick Kins and Anna Mary Henrich, maiden.

Koss, Elizabeth, of Joseph Koss and Mary Dopper, his wife, born January 11th, baptized March 30th. Sponsors, Joseph Aaron and Elizabeth Dopper, maiden.

Original book, page 52.

Noell, Michael, of Peter and Margaret Noell, born December 1st (evidently of the preceding year), baptized April 4th. Sponsors, Adam Kuhn and Mary Andress, maiden.

Peyfer, Peter, of George and Anna Peyfer, born August 9th (evidently of the preceding year), baptized May 25th. Sponsors, Henry Kuhn and Elizabeth Müller.

Schwerer, Nicholas, of Nicholas Schwerer and Catharine Garther, his wife, date of birth not given, baptized May 4th. Sponsors, James Meccful and Mary Schmidt.

Schwerer, Christina, of Nicholas and Catharine Schwerer, date of birth not given, baptized May 4th. Sponsors, Matthias Schmid and Elizabeth Henn.

Schwerer, Peter, of Nicholas and Catharine Schwerer, born September 7th, 1804, baptized May 4th. Sponsors, Peter Henn and Helen Meccfull [McFaul?].

Fields, Mary, of Philip and Catharine Fields, date of birth not given, baptized May 4th. Sponsors, Matthew Duff and Anna Fields.

Dagourthy [Dougherty?], John Benjamin, of James and Isabella Dagourthy, date of birth not given, baptized May 10th. Sponsors, Henry Monteck [Montague?] and Rose his wife.

O'Dannel, James, of Felix and Catharine O'Dannel, date of birth not given, baptized May 10th. Sponsors, John McQuire [McGuire?] and Mary Monteck [Montague?].

Merly, Sara, of James and Catharine Merly, date of birth not given, baptized May 10th. Sponsors, Michael and Bridget Dagourthy [Dougherty?].

Vorckman, Samuel Daniel, of Jacob and Mary Vorckman, date of birth not given, baptized May 17th. Sponsors, George Trox and Ann his wife.

Gelaspy [Gillespie?], Thomas, of Neil and Elizabeth Gelaspy, born March 26th, 1807, baptized May 17th. Sponsors, Edmund Borry and Susan Trox.

Meccedell, Elizabeth, of Patrick and Elizabeth Meccedell, date of birth not given, baptized May 17th. Sponsors, John Cannady [Kennedy?] and Elizabeth Therrin.

Aschman, Aaron, of William and Catharine Aschman, date of birth not given, baptized May 17th. Sponsors, John Kuhn and Mary Muller.

Meckeen [McKean?], Mary, of James Meckeen, twenty-one years of age, baptized May 27th and received into the church at the same time, having made her profession of Faith.

Cally [Kelly?], Mary, of John and Catharine Cally, date of birth not given, baptized May 24th. Sponsors, Edward Meccingly [McKinley] and Catharine his wife. (Then here follows the second entry of sponsors as Edward Meccingly and Bridget.)

Meccferrling, Edward, of Charles and Bridget Meccferling, date of birth not given, baptized May 24th. Sponsors, Daniel Boyl [Boyle?] and Catharine Meccferrling.

Carr, Crescentia, of Manasses and Catharine Carr, date of birth not given, baptized May 14th. Sponsors, John Hagerthy [Hagerty?] and Catharine Dugen.

Dugen, John, of John and Catharine Dugen, date of birth not given, baptized May 14th. Sponsors, Timothy and Petronilla Car.

Car [Carr?], Susan, of Patrick and Petronilla Car, date of birth not given, baptized May 14th. Sponsors, Hugo and Mary Boyl [Boyle?].

Mecgiven, Nicholas, of John and Mary McGiven, date of birth not given, baptized May 14th. Sponsors, John Meccferring and Susan Boyl [Boyle?].

Pathen [Patton?], Peter, of —— Pathen and Frances his wife, date of birth not given, baptized May 14th. Sponsors, Daniel and Genevieve Boyl [Boyle?].

Car [Carr?], Catharine, of Charles and Anna Car, date of birth not given, baptized May 14th. Sponsors, James Meccingly [McKinley?] and Catharine Galaugher.

Dagourthy, Petronilla, of Nicholas and Crescentia Dagourthy, date of birth not given, baptized May 14th. Sponsors, John and Mary Meccingly.

Meccbraid [McBride?], George Car, lawful son of Thomas and Mary Meccbraid, date of birth not given, baptized May 24th. Sponsors, Thomas Meccbraid and Mary Caster.

Hargens, William, of John and Bridget Hargens, born January 15th, baptized June 20th. Sponsors, Paul Doff and Bridget Meccdamerd [McDermott?].

O'Donner, Mary, of Daniel and Cecilia O'Donner, born October 16th, 1806, baptized July 19th. Sponsors, Patrick Meccdamert [McDermott?] and Ann Corrh......,

Patten, John, of James and Rachel Patten, born February 11th, baptized September 13th. Sponsors, John Burgoon and Mary his wife.

Ruffner, John, of George and Elizabeth Ruffner, born August 21st, baptized September 13th. Sponsors, John Henry and Elizabeth Ruffner.

Griffen, Andrew, of John and Mary Griffen, born November 3, 1806, baptized November 15th. Sponsors, George Ruffner and Sibylla his wife.

Dieder, Peter, of Henry and Catharine Dieder, born May 9th, baptized December 25th. Sponsors, Peter Muller and Catharine Dopper, maiden.

Griefen, Mary Magdalen, of Henry and Magdalen Griefen, born June 3d, baptized December 27th. Sponsors, Simon Ruffner and Catharine his wife.

1808

Magen, Margaret, of Bernard and Salome Magen, born March 29th (evidently of the preceding year), baptized January 10th. Sponsors, Henry Kuhn and Margaret Broun.

Dauff, ———, of Paul and Johanna Dauff, born August 8th (evidently of the preceding year), baptized January 18th. Sponsors, Philip Dauffy [Duffy?] and Margaret Corry, his wife.

Original book, page 55.

Wagener, Susan, of John and Barbara Wagener, born February 18th, baptized April 24th. Sponsors, Timothy Conner and Petronilla his wife.

Septer, Catharine, of Adam and Mary Septer, born December 12th (evidently of the preceding year), baptized April 24th. Sponsors, George and Elizabeth Ruffner.

Brick, John, of Henry and Elizabeth Brick, born January 14th, baptized April 24th. Sponsors, John Wagener and Barbara his wife.

O'Donnel, Hugo, of Daniel and Cecilia O'Donnel, born February 10th, baptized April 24th. Sponsors, Patrick McDarmer and Mary Roger.

Megardy [McCarthy?], Elizabeth, of Patrick and Elizabeth Megardy, three months old, baptized May 1st. Sponsors, John Mecannery and Eleanor his wife.

Mecadeny, John, of Peter and Bridget Mecadeny, born on the 29th (month and year not given), baptized May 1st. Sponsors, John Dagaurthy and Mary his wife.

Mecadeny, Bridget, of Peter and Bridget Mecadeny, four years old, baptized May 1st. Sponsors, Daniel Fields and Mary Quickly [Quigley?].

Fields, Elizabeth, of Philip and Catharine Fields, born 27th (month not given), 1807, baptized May 1st. Sponsors, Jacob Müller and Sara his wife.

Müller, Mary, of Jacob and Sara Müller, born August 28th, 1807, baptized May 1st. Sponsors, Balthasar Good and Martha Douff.

51

Good, John, of Balthasar and Rose Good, born March 20th, 1807, baptized May 1st. Sponsors, Matthew Schmidt and Elizabeth Elsner.

Original book, page 56.

May, Patrick, of Patrick and Mary May, born February 25th, 1808, baptized May 1st. Sponsors, William Porcker and Elizabeth Mequier [McGuire?].

Brennen, Timothy, of Michael and Mary Brennen, born July 14th, 1807, baptized May 1st. Sponsors, Christopher and Catharine Brennen.

O'Harra, Mary, of Philip and Catharine O'Harra, born February 25th, baptized May 1st. Sponsors, John Lochery and Mary O'Harra.

Thomas, Thomas, of William and Mary Thomas, born December 29th (evidently of the preceding year), baptized May 1st. Sponsors, Leonard Doppens and Salome Cifiny.

Meccfaull [McFaul?], James, of John and Mary Meccfaull, born February 29th, baptized May 1st. Sponsors, William Thomas and Petronilla Ross.

O'Brien, Mary, of Michael and Margaret O'Brien, born May 3d, baptized May 4th. Sponsors, William Forcker [Foraker?] and Anna his wife.

Meccaffry, Hugo, son of Hugo and Margaret Meccaffry, date of birth not given, baptized May 4th. Sponsors, Alexander May' and Cecilia his wife.

Rogers, Patrick, of Frank and Elizabeth Rogers, born January 14th, baptized May 6th. Sponsors, Samuel Montacc [Montague?] and Anna Broun [Brown?].

Haegens, Elizabeth, of Atur [Arthur?] and Mary Haegens, born July 19th (evidently of the preceding year), baptized May 8th. Sponsors, Timothy Broun [Brown?] and Anna Collerik.

Schinegen, Joseph, of John and Elizabeth Schinegen, born September 6th (evidently of the preceding year), baptized May 9th. Sponsors, Patrick Dannely [Donnelly?] and Eleanor Melon.

Meguy [McHugh?], Margaret, of John and Margaret Meguy, five years old, baptized May 15th. Sponsors, Felix Boyl [Boyle?] and Anna his wife.

Boyl [Boyle?] Agnes, of Felix and Anna Boyl, a year and a half old, baptized May 15th. Sponsors, Patrick Mequy [McKee?] and Anna his wife.

Lachery, Margaret, of Patrick and Anna Lachery, born March 14th, baptized May 15th. Sponsors, James Mecivestin and Anna his wife.

Reily, Mary, of Dionysius and Anna Reily, born May 17th (evidently of the preceding year), baptized May 15th. Sponsors, William Curry and Anna his wife.

Victor, Julia, of John and Mary Victor, born March 11th, baptized May 16th. Sponsors, George Trox and Anna his wife.

Megrady, Charles, of Patrick and Mary Megrady, born June 16th (evidently of the preceding year), baptized May 21st. Sponsors, Charles Flemming and Catharine his wife.

Mecbraid [McBride?], Margaret, of Hugo and Catharine Mecbraid, born July 29th (evidently of the preceding year), baptized May 21st. Sponsors, Anthony and Catharine Kelly.

Kelly, John, of Anthony and Catharine Kelly, born December 7th (evidently of the preceding year), baptized May 21st. Sponsors, Hugo and Catharine Mecbraid [McBride?].

Cary, Catharine, of Timothy and Susan Cary, born May 8th, baptized May 21st. Sponsors, Patrick and Sophie Meceelfrey.

Original book, page 57.

Ruffner, ———, son of George and Sibylla Ruffner, born February 2d, baptized May 26th. Sponsors, Simon and Catharine Ruffner.

Seywert [Seybert?], Rose, born January 21st, baptized May 29th. Sponsors, Joseph Boock and Rose his wife.

Trox, Amelia Anna, of Nicholas and Ruth Trox, born March 24th, baptized June 5th. Sponsors, John Borgoon [Burgoon?] and Mary his wife.

Merckell, Joseph, of John and Barbara Merckell, born April 6th, baptized June 5th. Sponsors, Jacob Henry and Margaret Syndorf.

Meccannell [McConnell?], Genevieve, of Jacob and Mary Meccannell, born February 15th, baptized June 5th. Sponsors, Timothy Conner and Margaret his daughter.

Borgoon, Joseph, of James and Martha Borgoon, born May 3d, baptized June 5th. Sponsors, James Mecquire [McGuire?] and Petronilla his wife.

Maholland [Mulholland?], Mary Ann, of David and Anna Maholland, born February 6th, baptized June 5th. Sponsors, Valentine Reinsell and Elizabeth his sister.

Handell, John, of Joseph and Mary Ann Handell, born May 10th, baptized June 5th. Sponsors, Dionysius Handell and Catharine his wife.

The following are from the month of May:

Goleagher [Gallagher?], John, of Anthony and Bridget Goleagher, born July 15th (evidently of the preceding year), baptized May 21st. Sponsors, Daniel Boyl and Susan Aron.

Ferry, Mary, of James and Catharine Ferry, born March 12th, baptized May 21st. Sponsors, John Meccginly [McKinly?] and Susan Galeagher [Gallagher?].

Morphy [Murphy?], Anna, of Terence and Margaret Morphy, born May 10th, baptized May 10. Sponsors, Charles Collerick and Mary Devin.

Meccginly [McKinley?], James, of James and Catharine Meccginley, born March 14th, baptized May 21st. Sponsors, James Hegerthy [Hagerty?] and Mary Dugen.

Meccferrien, Catharine, of John and Anna Meccferrien, nine years old, baptized May 21st. Sponsors, John and Catharine Meccferrien.

Galeagher [Gallagher?], Peter, of John and Mary Galeagher, born September 22d (evidently of the preceding year), baptized May 21st. Sponsors, Edward Mecgirley and Bridget his wife.

Coll, Crescentia, of James and Salome Coll, born May 27th (evidently of the preceding year), baptized May 21st. Sponsors, Patrick Boyl and Crescentia Galeagher [Gallagher?].

Dagcarthy [Dougherty?], Eleazer, of Lochly and Salome Dagcarthy, born August 31st (evidently of the preceding year), baptized June 12th. Sponsors, George Zinsdorff and Susan, his sister.

Ferrell, Anna, of Cornelius and Margaret Ferrell, born May 16th, baptized June 12th. Sponsors, John Borgoon and Mary his wife.

Müller, George, of Martin and Magdalene Müller, born May 27th, baptized July 3d. Sponsors, Conrad Henry and Elizabeth Maller.

Konnly [Conley?], Peter, of Eiden Konnly and Mary Lacheren, born December 2d, 1807, baptized August 15th. Sponsors, R. P. Helbron and Mary Wight.

Ruffner, Peter, of Simon and Mary Barbara Ruffner, born August 3d, baptized August 28th. Sponsors, George Ruffner and Sibylla, his wife.,

Megill [McGill?], Susan, of James and Bridget Megill, born June 24th, baptized August 28th. Sponsors, Jacob Hoeny and Catharine, a maiden.

Bivers, Susan, of Thomas and Elizabeth Bivers, born July 15th, baptized August 28th. Sponsors, Simon Noel and Susan Zinsdorf.

Noell, Margaret, of Joseph and Margaret Noell, born June 25th, baptized September 4th. Sponsors, Simon Ruffner and Margaret Griffy.

Meckelfy, James, of Patrick and Anna Meckelfy, born July 28th, baptized September 4th. Sponsors, Patrick Dauffy and Elizabeth Seyfert.

Mechachen, Sara, of Arthur and Margaret Mechachen, seven years old, baptized October 9th. Sponsors, John Wight and Theresa his wife.

Mechachen, Andrew, son of the same father, baptized October 9th. Sponsor, George Ruffner.

Mechachen, James, another son of the same father, seven years old, baptized October 9th. Sponsor, John Kelly.

Mechachen, Joseph, another son of the same father, five months old, baptized October 9th. Sponsors, Joseph Schmidt and Mary his wife.

Mechachen, Elizabeth, another daughter of the same father, four years old, baptized October 9th. Sponsors, Christian Ruffner and Catharine his wife.

Mechachen, Mary, another daughter of the same father, two years old, baptized October 9th. Sponsors, Jacob Allwein and Catherine, his wife.

Ruffner, Susan, of Christian and Mary Ruffner, born August 16th, baptized October 9th. Sponsors, John Wight and Theresa his wife.

Broccley, Bridget, of Patrick and Petronilla Broccley, 11 years old, baptized October 9th. Sponsors, Patrick Canrowe and his wife.

Pett, Mary, of Henry and Mary Pett, three years old, baptized October 9th. Sponsors, Michael Wiht with his wife.

Thernan, Michael, of Michael and Elizabeth Thernan, five months old, baptized by R. D. O'Brien on November 1st. Sponsors, Patrick Mecschiveston and Mary Laighton.

Mecary, Elizabeth, of James and Anna Mecary, five years old, baptized November 6th. Sponsors, Balthasar Good and Helen his wife.

Original book, page 60.

Murry, Mary, of James and Anna Murry, three years old, baptized November 6th. Sponsors, Alexander May and Margaret Mecady.

Gother, Jacob, of Thomas and Mary Gother, one year old, baptized November 6th. Sponsors, William Porcy and Anna Morphy.

Kuhn, Mary, of John and Sara Kuhn, eleven months old, baptized November 6th. Sponsors, John Mecfaull and Martha his wife.

Kuhn, Samuel, of John and Sara Kuhn, two years old, baptized November 6th. Sponsors, Christian Brannen and Mary Hugy.

Galgher [Gallagher?], James, of Martin and Margaret Galgher, five months old, baptized November 6th. Sponsors, Charles Wickley [Weakland?] and Elizabeth his wife.

Collen, William, of Patrick and Catharine Collen, three months old, baptized November 6th. Sponsors, William O'Hara and Eleanor Kelly.

May, Bernard, of Alexander and Cecilia May, two months old, baptized November 6th. Sponsors, Daniel Morphy and Elizabeth his wife.

Mecanny, Margaret, of John and Helen Mecanny, four months old, baptized November 7th. Sponsors, Jacob Thull and Sabina Wickson.

Thull, Jacob, of Jacob and Sabina Thull, one year old, baptized November 7th. Sponsors, Patrick Duff and Helen Mecanny.

FATHER PETER HELBRON'S GREENSBURG, PA., REGISTER

Copied from the original by the Rev. Father John, O. S. B., of Saint Vincent's Abbey, Pennsylvania. Translated by Lawrence F. Flick, M.D., L.L.D.

1809

Curry, Daniel, of John and Margaret Curry, born January 28th, baptized by R. D. O'Bryan, April 2d. Sponsors, Jacob Kuhn and Margaret Coll.

Hargens, Catharine, of John and Bridget Hargens, born March 11th, baptized by R. D. O'Bryen, April 3d. Sponsors, Charles Roger and Bridget McDarmeth [McDermott?].

Original book, page 61.

Brick, Peter, of Peter and Margaret Brick, born March 22d, 1809, baptized April 16th. Sponsors, Peter Ruffner and Elizabeth Brick.

[N*95.—In the original "by the same" is constantly used, and refers to Father Helbron. Father Helbron really copied the records into the book even of the baptisms of Father O'Brien, the latter in all probability furnishing him the notes. This is indicated by the manner in which the Irish names have been spelled and in which Father O'Brien's own name has been spelled.—L. F. F.]

Campbell, Andrew, of Michael and Sibylla Campbell, born November 9th (evidently of the preceding year), baptized April 30th. Sponsors, Anthony Campbell and Mary Campbell, maiden.

Riffel, Thomas, of Bernard and Margaret Riffel, born December 6th, 1801, baptized April 30th. No sponsors given.

Riffel, Michael, born May 17th, 1804, of the same father.

Riffel, Abraham, born December 24th, 1805, of the same father.

Riffel, Elizabeth, born May 26th, 1808. No sponsors given for any of them.

Mecenaldy, Sara and Anna Maria, of —— Mecenaldy and Catharine his wife. Sara born August 10th, date of birth of Anna Maria not given but probably the same date, baptized April 30th. Sponsors, Neal Meclansy and Rose Koyl [Coyle?].

Koyl [Coyle?], Terence, of Philip and Catharine Koyl, four years old, baptized April 30th. Sponsors, Peter Meccenaldy and Isabel Campbell.

Koyl, Andrew, four months old, baptized (presumably on the same day). Sponsors, Charles Roger and Catharine Campbell.

Denaho [Donahoe], John and Anna, of John and Genevieve Denaho (date of birth not given), baptized by the same May 5th. Sponsors, Cornelius and Anna Mecdonnell.

Hammer, Joseph, of John and Margaret Hammer (date of birth not given), baptized May 5th. Sponsors, Mary Schmid and Patrick Mecdonnell.

Sander, John, of John and Mary Sander, born July 27th (evidently of the preceding year), baptized May 7th. Sponsors, James Mecdonnell and Margaret Koss.

Koss, Henry, of Joseph and Mary Koss, born May 22d, baptized May 24th. Sponsors, Henry Reinsel and Elizabeth his wife.

Mecdarmet [McDermott?], William, of Patrick and Bridget Mecdarmet, born April 9th, baptized June 1st. Sponsors, George Trox and ——— Prudy, maiden.

Original book, page 62.

Borgoon, John, of Barnabas and Mary Borgoon, born May 13th, baptized July 31st. Sponsors, George Trox and Margaret Pettecult.

Brucher, Agnes, of Charles and Agnes Brucher, born May 1st, baptized July 16th. Sponsors, Peter and Catharine Rogers.

Hoeny, John, of John and Susan Hoeny, born July 13th, baptized August 27th. Sponsors, John and Petronilla Conner.

Mecmolland, Margaret, of Inos and Catharine Mecmolland, born April 7th, baptized August 27th. Sponsors, Christopher Glass and Margaret his wife.

Hürsman, Theresa, of John and Mary Hürsman, born August 5th, baptized September 1st. Sponsors, Matthias and Margaret Brick.

Dagharty [Dougherty?], Thomas, of Lachelin and Sallie Dagharty, born March 9th, baptized September 1st. Sponsors, John Wagener and Barbara his wife.

Haas, Salome, of Samuel and Barbara Haas, born April 9th, baptized September 10th. Sponsors, Henry and Margaret Brick.

Kelly, John, of Patrick and Margaret Kelly, born March 30th, baptized September 23d. Sponsors, John Grünewald and Catharine Dopper.

[NOTE.—In this entry the plural verb "baptizati sunt" is used, although the name of only one child is given.]

Kelly, Margaret, of Patrick and Margaret Kelly, born February 7th, 1805, baptized September 23d. Sponsors, John Henrich and Mary Grünewald.

Cafferty, John, of John and Mary Cafferty, born February 10th, baptized September 25th. Sponsors, Patrick Mequire [McGuire?] and Margaret Hergens.

Armstrong, Frances, born January 12th, baptized September 25th. Sponsors, Patrick Mequire and Frances his wife.

Gryffen, Margaret, of John and Mary Gryffen, born September 29th, 1809, baptized October 15th. Sponsors, Simon and Catharine Ruffner.

Meglachlen [McLaughlin?], Catharine, of Nicholas Meglachlen and Pity, his wife, born October 22d, baptized at Carlistle on November 12th. Sponsors, Edward Pentegrass and Mary Jonshten.

Glass, William, of Christopher and Margaret Glass, born October 23d, baptized December 3d. Sponsors, Dionysius and Mary Conner.

Reinsel, Margaret, of Henry and Elizabeth Reinsel, born October 11th, baptized December 3d. Sponsors, George Reinsel and Margaret Dopper.

Ruffner, John, of George and Sibylla Ruffner, born August 17th, 1809, baptized December 24th. Sponsors, William Dagourthy and Margaret his wife.

Kuhn, Peter, of George and Mary Kuhn, born November 29th, 1809, baptized December 25th. Sponsors, Peter Aaren and Mary his wife.

Kinz, Anna Mary, of Frederick and Mary Kinz, born November 26th, 1809, baptized December 25th. Sponsors, John Henry and Mary Barbara his wife.

1810

Noell, Henry, of Peter and Margaret Noell, born December 18th, baptized March 4th. Sponsors, Philip Seyverth [Seybert?] and Barbara his wife.

Conner, John, of Dionysius and Mary Conner, born January 16th, baptized March 11th. Sponsors, Timothy Conner and Petronilla his wife.

Merckell, Mary Ann, of John and Barbara Merckell, born December 8th, baptized March 18th. Sponsors, Frederick Kyns and Mary his wife.

Ruffner, Mary Ann, of George and Elizabeth Ruffner, born September 2d (evidently of the preceding year), baptized April 15th. Sponsors, John Grünewald and Mary Andress.

O'Donnel, Bridget, of Daniel and Cecilia O'Donnel, born December 3d (evidently of the preceding year), baptized April 19th. Sponsors, John Roger and Cecilia his wife.

Seyvert [Seybert?], Julia, of Philip and Elizabeth Seyvert, born November 4th (evidently of the preceding year), baptized by the same April 22d. Sponsors, Philip Seyvert and Barbara his wife.

Müller, Anna, of Martin and Magdalen Müller, born March 2d, baptized April 22d. Sponsors, Thomas Aaron and Anna Mulleni, widow.

Original book, page 65.

Ruffner, Henry and Peter, brothers, of George and Susan Ruffner, date of birth not given, baptized April 23d. Sponsors, George Ruffner and Anna Maria, his wife, for the one, and Peter Simon Ruffner and Anna Maria Zinsdorff for the other.

Kuhn, Mary Elizabeth, of Henry and Catharine Kuhn, born March 28th, baptized April 23d. Sponsors, Henry Reinzell and Elizabeth his wife.

Arens, George, of Peter and Mary Arens, born April 7th, baptized April 29th. Sponsors, George Kuhn and Mary his wife, for whom Catharine Dopper stood as proxy.

Handel, Catharine, of Dionysius and Catharine Handel, born February 2d, baptized May 6th. Sponsors, Catharine Zinsdorff, maiden, and Conrad Henry.

Kuhn, John, of Jacob and Mary Kuhn, born May 1st, baptized June 3d. Sponsors, George Ruffner and Mary his wife.

Michen [Meehan?], Sara, of Bernard and Sallie Michen, born June 1st, 1809, baptized by the same June 3d. Sponsors, Jacob Ruffner and Margaret Broun.

Noell, Anna, of Joseph and Margaret Noell, born March 12th, baptized July 15th. Sponsors, John Henry and Mary Henrich his wife.

Zepter [Septer?], John, of Adam and Mary Zepter, born April 20th, 1809, baptized July 15th. Sponsors, Simon Ruffner and Catharine his wife.

Original book, page 66.

Schorts, Margaret, of John and Anna Schorts, born January 10th, baptized July 15th. Sponsors, Jacob Hoeny and Elfy Coogen.

Megouhh [McGough?], James, of John and Sara Megouhh, born June 23d, baptized July 15th. Sponsors, Jacob Reyhen and Susan Drox, maiden.

Ruffner, Daniel, of Christian and Mary Ruffner, born January 23d, baptized July 29th. Sponsors, George Ruffner and Mary his wife.

Molling, Mary, of Richard and Annabel Molling, born February 30th, baptized August 15th. Sponsors, John Roger and Catharine Roger his mother.

Mecdarmor, Mary, of Patrick and Bridget Mecdarmor, born August 18th (evidently of the preceding year), baptized August 15th. Sponsors, Jacob Hoeny and Margaret Collfy.

Griffy, Henry, of Henry and Magdalen Griffy, born July 14th, baptized October 14th. Sponsors, George Ruffner and Margaret Isly [Easly?].

Handell, Joseph, of Joseph and Mary Handell, born April 27th, baptized October 21st. Sponsors, Peter Ruffner and Margaret Ruffner.

Ruffner, Henry, of Henry and Elizabeth Ruffner, born August 1st, baptized October 28th. Sponsors, Simon Ruffner and Mary Barbara his wife.

Morx [Marx?], John, of Jacob and Theresa Morx, born October 14th, baptized November 1st. Sponsors, Matthias Brick and Mary his daughter.

Original book, page 67.

Britge, George Henry, of Henry and Elizabeth Britge, born August 13th, baptized November 1st. Sponsors, George Henry Reinzell and Elizabeth his wife.

Megennery [McEnery?], Mary, of John and Mary Megennery, born October 26th, baptized December 2d. Sponsors, John Roger and Mary McDarmer.

Carr, Frances, of Manasses and Catharine Carr, born May 2d, baptized at the River Yock, November 25th. Sponsors, William McQuinly and Anna his sister.

Coll, Anna, of James and Salome Coll, two years old, baptized December 25th. Sponsors, Daniel Boyl and Cecilia his wife.

Callaigher, Mary, of John and Mary Callaigher, born August 18th, baptized December 25th. Sponsors, Dionysius and Catharine Dugen.

Brick, Andrew, of Peter and Margaret Brick, born November 30th, baptized December 25th. Sponsors, Jacob Kuhn and Mary Ruffner.

1811

Conner, James, of Dionysius and Mary Conner, date of birth not given, baptized March 29th. Sponsors, James Megeel and Catharine Kuhn.

Ruffner, Catharine, of Simon and Mary Barbara Ruffner, born December 9th, 1810, baptized April 11th. Sponsors, George Kuhn and Mary his wife.

Mecfee, Salome, of Patrick and Anna Mecfee, born November 9th (evidently of the preceding year), baptized April 14th. Sponsors, Frank Gilde [Guilday?] and Anna Thomas.

Carr, Manasses, of Patrick and Petronilla Carr, born February 22d, baptized June 2d. Sponsors, Daniel Boyl and Catharine Dugen.

Calegar [Gallagher?], Frances, of Anthony and Bridget Calegar, born May 24th, baptized June 2d. Sponsors, James and Julia Boyl.

Grenewald [Grünwald?], Catharine, of Joseph and Mary Grenewald, born October 24th, 1810, baptized June 13th. Sponsors, Henry Brick and Elizabeth his wife.

Hargen, Mary, of Nicholas and Bridget Hargen, born February 7th, baptized July 7th. Sponsors, John Hargen and Catharine Roger.

Borgoon [Burgoon?], Elizabeth, of Bernard and Mary Borgoon, born April 21st, baptized July 14th. Sponsors, Peter Corrigen and Prudy his wife.

Pettecott, Salome, of Jacob and Margaret Pettecott, eight months old, baptized July 14th. Sponsors, Michael Corrigen and Anna Welsch.

Septer, Christina, of Adam and Mary Septer, born June 28th, baptized August 26th. Sponsors, Simon Noell and Mary Andreas [Andrews?].

Ruffner, Catharine, of George and Sibylla Ruffner, born May 14th, baptized August 8th. Sponsors, Ferdinand Isly [Easly?] and Margaret his wife.

Brugen, Mary, of Charles and Agnes Brugen, born September 9th, baptized October 6th. Sponsors, John Wagener and Barbara his wife.

Isly [Easly?], Johanna, of Anthony and Elizabeth Isly, born September 1st, baptized Otober 28th. Sponsors, Jacob Kuhn and Mary his wife.

1812

Glass, Jacob, of Christopher and Margaret Glass, born January 2d, baptized January 2d. Sponsors, John Hoeny and Catharine. (No further designation.)

Kuhn, Joseph, of Jacob and Mary Kuhn, born December 21st, 1810, baptized February 9th. Sponsors, Peter Brick and Margaret his wife.

Müller, Magdalen, of Martin and Magdalen Müller, born November 9th, 1811, baptized February 16th. Sponsors, James Henrich and Margaret Zinsdorff, widow.

Kins, Barbara, of Frederick and Mary Kins, born October 7th, 1811, baptized February 23d. Sponsors, James Henry, a young man and Mary Kins, maiden.

Morfy [Murphy?], Margaret, of Neil and Margaret Morfy, born January 26th, baptized March 29th. Sponsors, Patrick Morfy and Margaret his wife.

Hirsman, Mary, of John and Mary Hirsman, born January 10th, baptized March 25th. Sponsors, Matthias Brick and Mary his wife.

Ruffner, Salome, of Christian and Mary Ruffner, born December 6th (evidently of the preceding year), baptized March 25th. Sponsors, Peter Ruffner and Rose Wight.

FATHER PETER HELBRON'S GREENSBURG, PA., REGISTER

Copied from the original by the Rev. Father, John, O. S. B., of Saint Vincent's Abbey, Pennsylvania. Translated by Lawrence F. Flick, M.D., LL.D.

1812—CONTINUED

Mercckel (Christian name of child not given), daughter of John and Anna Barbara Mercckel, born January 25th, baptized April 12th. Sponsors, John Henry and Mary Barbara his wife.

Mecfee, Elizabeth, of Patrick and Anna Mecfee, born January 29th, baptized April 12th. Sponsors, James Megee and Bridget his wife.

THE CONGREGATION AT BOFFLOE

O'Dannel, Patrick, of Dionysius and Margaret O'Dannel, born February 27th, baptized April 26th. Sponsors, Patrick Ried and Anna Braun.

Original book, page 70.

Gelaspy [Gillespie?], James, of Nicholas and Barbara Gelaspy, born November 29th, baptized April 26th. Sponsors, James Mecbraidt and Barbara his wife.

Beyly [Bailey?], Hugo, of Patrick and Catharine Beyly, born March 16th, baptized April 26th. Sponsors, John Quinn and Anna Meguy [Magee?].

Meclachelen [McLaughlin?], Bernard, of Patrick and Anna Meclachelen, born January 14th, baptized April 26th. Sponsors, John Boil and Mary his wife.

O'Donnel, Michael, of Nicholas and Bridget O'Donnel, born January 19th, baptized April 26th. Sponsors, Peter Dogen and Margaret McColl.

Cary [Carey?], Rose, of Timothy and Susan Cary, born December 20th (evidently of the preceding year), baptized April 26th. Sponsors, Nicholas Dogen and Margaret Scherethon [Sheridan?].

Meccfy, Hugo, of Daniel and Bridget Meccfy, born March 9th, baptized April 26th. Sponsors, John Duffy and Sara Hartman.

Froilet, William, of John and Cecilia Froilet, born September 21st (evidently of the preceding year), baptized April 26th. Sponsors, James and Bridget Quinn.

Meccelray [McElroy?], Mary, of Charles and Mary Meccelray, born October 2d (evidently of the preceding year), baptized April 26th. Sponsors, Patrick Gelaspy [Gillespie?] and Mary Preys.

Migen, Patrick, of John and Rachel Migen, date of birth not given, baptized April 26th. Sponsors, Alexander Hagerthy and Margaret. (No further designation.)

Megarthy [McCarthy?], John, of John and Anna Megarthy, born February 3d, baptized April 26th, Sponsors, Dionysius and Susan Dogen.

O'Donnel, Dionysius, of Cornelius and Elizabeth O'Donnel, born January 12th, baptized April 26th. Sponsors, John Gelaspy and Bridget Duffy.

Mecdemard, Salome, of Patrick and Bridget Mecdemard, born December 17th (evidently of the preceding year), baptized April 26th. Sponsors, Nicholas Mecbraigdt and Salome Dogen.

Dogen, Daniel, of Michael and Bridget Dogen, born March 8th, baptized April 26th. Sponsors, Dionysius O'Donnel and Bridget his wife.

Mecbraigd [McBride?], Nicholas, of Nicholas and Sibylla Mecbraigd, born February 1st, baptitzed April 26th. Sponsors, Marck Meguy [McHugh?] and Mary his wife.

Original book, page 71.

Ruffner, Susan, of George and Susan Ruffner, born April 8th, baptized May 7th. Sponsors, Peter Ruffner and Susan Handell.

Aaron, Margaret, of Peter and Mary Aaron, born March 24th, baptized May 7th. Sponsors, John Gery and Elizabeth Zinsdorff.

Kenann [Keenan?], Rebecca and Rose, of Jacob and Catharine Kenann (date of birth not given), baptized by Father Megeer [McGirr?] May 23d. Sponsors, Peter Arens, with his wife, and Terence Megeer and Catharine, daughter of Ferdinand Isly [Easly?[.

Litz, Catharine, of Daniel and Catharine Litz, five years old, baptized May 30th. Sponsors, George Reinzell and Catharine Dapper.

Spring, John, of Joseph and Susan Spring, born October 26th, 1811, baptized May 30th. Sponsors, John Henrich and Mary Barbara. (No further designation.)

Molline [Mullin?], Salome, of Dionysius and Catharine Molline, born April 17th, 1811, baptized May 30th. Sponsors, John McGough and Sara his wife.

Kelly, Genevieve, of John and Ella Kelly, born October 8th (evidently of the preeeding year), baptized July 5th. Sponsors, Henry Kuhn and Catharine his wife.

Peas, John, of Jacob and Catharine Peas, born May 18th, baptized July 5th. Sponsors, John Gerry and Elizabeth Seyfert [Seybert?].

Conner, Salome, of Dionysius and Magdalen Conner, born June 11th, baptized July 5th. Sponsors, Jacob Hoeny and Petronilla Conner.

Thiter, Susan, of Henry and Catharine Thiter, born October 27th (evidently of the preceding year), baptized July 26th. Sponsors, John Henrich and Elizabeth Muller.

Roger, Joseph, of John and Cecilia Roger, born August 8th, baptized September 26th. Sponsors, William Dagourthy and Margaret his wife.

O'Donnel, Elizabeth, of Daniel and Cecilia O'Donnel, born December 1st (evidently of the preceding year), baptized October 18th. Sponsors, Christian Ruffner and Elizabeth Noell.

Schorth [Short?], Mary Ann, of John and Anna Schorth, born March 14th, baptized October 18th. Sponsors, Peter Carrigan and Prudentia his wife.

Kuhn, Salome, of George and Mary Kuhn, born on the 7th (month not given), baptized October 25th. Sponsors, Jacob Kuhn and Catharine his sister.

Pettecorth, Jacob, of Jacob and Margaret Pettecorth, born May 15th, baptized October 25th. Sponsors, Livey Borgoon and Mary Bertly.

Borgoon [Burgoon?], Dionysius, of James and Margaret Borgoon, born October 8th, baptized November 1st. Sponsors, Peter Carrigan and Prudentia his wife.

Griffy, Catharine, of John and Mary Griffy, born May 13th, baptized November 22d. Sponsors, Henry Griffen and Magdalen his wife.

Huntsberger, Daniel, of Peter and Catharine Huntsberger, born November 20th, baptized November 22d. Sponsors, Philip Seiffert and Barbara his wife.

Doff [Duff?], Rose, of Paul and Johanna Doff, born July 29th, four years old, baptized December 17th. Sponsors, John Curren and Margaret his wife.

1813

Brick, Susanna, of Peter and Margaret Brick, born January 5th, baptized February 25th. . Sponsors, George Kuhn and Mary his wife.

———, (Family name not given), Hugh, born 1811 (day of birth not given) son, and Bibina his sister, three years old, daughter of the same father, baptized by the same April 11th. Sponsors, Moyses Gilaspy and Anna May.

McGill, William, of James and Bridget McGill, born February 4th, baptized by the same May 2nd. Sponsors, John Hoeny and Susan his wife.

Wight [White?], Thomas, born November 15th (evidently of the preceding year) baptized by the same May 2nd. Sponsors, John Wegth and Theresa, his wife.

Duff, John, of Paul and Johanna Duff, born February 20th, baptized
by the same May 9th. Sponsors, Patrick Mecbarn and Catharine Roger.

Muller, Daniel, of Martin and Magdalen Muller, born April 10th, baptized by the same May 16th. Sponsors, John Henrich and Mary
his wife.

Original book, page 74.

Hemler, Christian, of Christian Hemler and Catharine his wife, born
May 8th, baptized by the same July 10th. Sponsors, Adam Staudt
and Elizabeth Zinsdorff.

Madje, Arthur, of William Madje and Mary, his wife, born November
8th (evidently of the preceding year), baptized July 10th. Sponsors, John Kelly and Elizabeth Holder.

Mecdonnell, Anna, of Dionysius and Cecilia Mecdonnell, born April
8th, baptized by the same August 1st. Sponsors, John Roger and
Cecilia, his wife.

Wagener, Elizabeth, of John Wagener and Barbara, his wife, born
June 5th, baptized by the same August 1st. Sponsors, Henry
Reinzell and Elizabeth, his wife.

Patten, William, of James Patten and Rachel, his wife, born June 5th,
baptized by the same August 15th. Sponsors, Daniel Boyl and
Bridget Patten.

Monholland [Mulhollond?], Eleanor, of David Monholland and Anna
his wife, born February 6th, baptized by the same August 22nd.
Sponsors, Jacob Hoeny and Elizabeth Mecciven [McIvan?].

Burgoon, Barbara, of Bernard Burgoon and Mary, his wife, date of
birth not given, baptized by the same August 24th. Sponsors,
Peter Korrien and Petronilla. Surname not given.

1810

[The following entries are made on page 74 of the original book but
are distinctly marked 1810. Evidently they were entered from a memorandum. L. F. F.]

Moore, Peter, of David Moore and Sarah, his wife; five years old,
baptized by the same (month not given but possiby August) 12th.
Sponsors, David Cannady [Kennedy?] and Catharine Cannady,
his sister.

Moore, Sarah, of David Moore and Sarah, his wife; twelve years old,
baptized by the same on the same day. Sponsors, Balthasar Good
and Agnes Mayo.

Moore, James, of David Moore and Sarah, his wife; eight years old,
baptized by the same (evidently on the same day) although not
stated. Sponsors, John Schmidt and Margaret his wife.

Meclaglen [McLaughlin?], James,. of Michael Meclaglen and Rose, his
wife, baptized by the same on the same day with three others baptized by the same priest, that is, with Mary, Anna and William
and with the same sponsors.

Original book, page 75.

Kuhn, Jacob, of Jacob Kuhn and Mary, his wife, born on the tenth
day of the same month, baptized by the same on October 31st. It
is uncertain whether in 1810 or 1813, but probably in 1813. Sponsors, Solomon Kuhn and Margaret Brick.

(Note: The following entry for December stands both under 1813
and the year 1810 but inasmuch as 1810 is evidently an insert for the
few extra baptisms of August, we may assume that the December
entry is for 1813. L. F. F.)

Molling, Catharine, of Richard Molling and Isabel, his wife, born
July 14, baptized by the same, December 10th. Sponsors, Peter
Carrien and Prudentia, his wife.

(The entries which follow are for October and September, probably
of 1813 although they likewise stand under the heading of 1810.
L. F. F.)

Brick, Margaret, of Henry Brick and Elizabeth his wife; date of
birth not given, baptized by the same October 9th. Sponsors,
George Brick and Margaret, his sister.

Gerry, Samuel, of John and Catharine, his wife; date of birth not
given, baptized by the same on the 19th of the same month. (Evidently October.) Sponsors, Martin Gerry and Mary, his wife.

Bracken, Helen, of Charles Bracken and Agnes, his wife, born on the
twelfth of September, baptized by the same on the same day (evidently as the preceding one). Sponsors, John Conner and Helen,
his sister.

Reinzel, Elizabeth, of George Reinzel and Catharine, his wife; date
of birth not given, baptized September 18th. Sponsors, Henry
Reinzel and Elizabeth, his wife.

Kinz, Conrad, of Frederick Kinz and Mary, his wife, born November
5th, baptized by the same on the 19th. (Probably of December).
Sponsors, Conrad Henry and Mary Kinz.

Conner, William, of Dionysius Conner and Magdalen, his wife, born
October 27th, baptized by the same the 25th. (Probably of December). Sponsors, Solomon Kuhn and Elizabeth Breiht.

1814.

Aaron, Elizabeth, of Joseph Aaron and Margaret, his wife, born on
the same day, baptized by the same on the 9th. (Month not
given). Sponsors, Peter Brick and Margaret, his wife.

Brick, Cornelius, born November 18th (evidently of the preceding year), baptized February 2nd. Sponsors, John Hiersman and his wife.

Original book, page 76.

Miller, John, of George Miller and Catharine, his wife, born March 30th, baptized by the same April 7th. Sponsors, Andrew Gerstenweiler and Anna Maria Zinsdorff.

Drux, Susan, of George Drux and Bridget, his wife, born October, 25th, baptized by the same April 10th. Sponsors, Abraham Drux and Bridget McDemord, maiden.

Ruffner, Catharine, of Simon Ruffner and Mary Barbara, his wife, born December 14, 1813, baptized by the same April 11th. Sponsors, William Daugherty and Margaret, his wife.

Kuhns, Solomon, of George Kuhns and Mary, his wife, born March 20th, baptized by the same April 17th. Sponsors, Solomon Kuhn and Mary Harry, maiden.

Gery, Bridget, of Martin Gery and Mary his wife, born January 31st, baptized by the same April 17th. Sponsors, Peter Ruffner and Theresa Cread.

Gryffen, [Griffin?], Margaret, of Henry Griffin and Mary, his wife, born June 6th, (evidently of the preceding year) baptized by the same April 17th. Sponsors, Jacob Kuhn and Mary, his wife.

Ruffner, Catharine, of George Ruffner and Susan, his wife, born March 16th, baptized by the same (date not given, but probably April 17th). Sponsors, Joseph Zinsdorff and Catharine Ruffner.

Schmidt, Elizabeth, of Joseph Schmidt and Catharine, his wife, born January 17th, baptized by the same, April 24th. Sponsors, John Bornheimer and Elizabeth Handell.

Arens, Joseph, of Peter Arens and Mary, his wife, born May 30th, baptized by the same June 2nd. Sponsors, Mosses Gelaspy and Theresa Cred.

Molliry, William, of Bernard Molliry and Susan his wife, born September 5th, (evidently of the preceding year), baptized by the (date not given, but probably June 2nd). Sponsors, Michael Meciver [McIvor?], and Elizabeth Megiver.

Müller, Rose, of Peter Müller and Mary, his wife; two years old, baptized by the same in July (date not given). Sponsors, Joseph Bock and Rose.

Original book, page 77.

Kelly, Edward, of John Kelly and Ally, his wife, born October 9th, baptized by the same July 3rd. Sponsors, John Roger and Cecilia, his wife.

Cred, Johanna, of Daniel Cred and Salome, his wife, born March 20th, baptized by the same, July 17th. Sponsors, Thomas Aroon and Theresa Cred.

Megrady, Clemens, of Patrick Megrady and Mary, his wife; five years old, baptized by the same on July 31st. Sponsors, Clement Burleigh and Cecilia Roger.

Meckelfee, Daniel, of Patrick Meckelfee and Anna, his wife, born March 15th, baptized by the same August 14th. Sponsors, Mosses Gilasby and Salome Laden.

Borgoon, James, of Livey and Anna, his wife, born July 3rd, baptized by the same August 15th. Sponsors, Edward Delany and Margaret Megouht.

Morphy, John, of Patrick Morphy and Amelia, his wife; two years old, on September 29th, baptized by the same August 28th. Sponsors, Patrick Megraty and Amelia Morphy.

——, Margaret (family name not given) of —— and Mary, his wife; three years old on August 20th, baptized by the same on August 28th. Sponsors, Patrick Morphy and Catharine Isly.

Machen, Harriet, of Martin Machen and Salome, his wife, born January 22nd, 1814, baptized by the same October 23rd. Sponsors, Joseph Handel and Margaret Broun.

Handel, Aloysius, of Joseph Handel and Mary, his wife, born September, 1813, baptized by the same October 23rd. Sponsors, Dionysius Handel and Salome Machen.

Original book, page 78.

Henrich, John, of John Henrich and Mary, his wife, born October 30th, baptized by the same November 10th. Sponsors, John Henrich and Barbara, his wife.

Hirsman, John, of John Hirsman and Mary, his wife, born June 16th, baptized by the same November 20th. Sponsors, James Henry and Elizabeth Brick.

Kuhn, Andrew, of Jacob Kuhn and Mary, his wife, born November 4th, baptized by the same, December 11th. Sponsors, Andrew Gerstenweiler and Catharine, his wife.

Grunewaldt, John, of John Grunewaldt and Anna, his wife, born December 6th, baptized by the same December 25th. Sponsors, William Dagourthy and Margaret, his wife.

Merckell, Conrad, of John Merckell and Barbara, his wife, born August 11th, baptized by the same December 26th. Sponsors, Conrad Henry and Mary Kinz.

1815.

Brick, Matthias, of Peter Brick and Margaret, his wife, born December 26th, baptized by the same January 15th. Sponsors, Andrew Gerstenweiler and Catharine, his wife.

Wight, [White?], Mary Magdalen, of George Wight and Elizabeth, his wife, born January 1st, baptized by the same February 12th. Sponsors, James Noell and Rose Wight.

Hunsberger, Elizabeth, of Peter Hunsberger and Catharine, his wife, born January 5th, baptized by the same March 12th. Sponsors, Daniel Cred and Salome, his wife.

O'Donnel, James, of Daniel O'Donnel and Cecilia his wife, born November 16th, baptized by the same March 12th. Sponsors, Timothy Conner and Petronilla Conner.

Original book, page 79.

Massereo, Israel, of Israel Massereo and Mary, his wife, born February 21st, baptized by the same April 9th. Sponsors, Peter Ruffner and Margaret Zinsdorff.

Noell, Margaret, of Simon Noell and Mary, his wife, born March 5th, baptized by the same, April 9th. Sponsors, Peter Noell and Margaret, his wife.

Ruffner, George, of George Ruffner and Sibylla, his wife, born February 15th, baptized by Rev. G. F. X. O'Brien April 12th. Sponsors, James and Mary Eastly. (Written by Rev. O'Brien, P.J., O.S.B).

Roger, William, of John Roger and Cecilia, his wife, born March 20th, baptized by the same April 16th. Sponsors, Moses Gelaspy and Mary Coll.

Reinzel, Daniel of George Reinzel and Catherine, his wife, born March 12th, baptized by the same April 16. Sponsors, Henry Reinzel and Catherine Kuhn.

Dulany, Margaret, of Dennis Dulany and Margaret, his wife, born February 17th, baptized by Rev. G. F. X. O'Brien April 16th. Sponsors, John Rogers and Anna MecAfee. (Written by Rev. G. F. X. O'Brien, P.J., O.S.B.).

McClean, George, of John McClean and Rose, his wife, born on the 26th (month not given) 1813, baptized by the same May 7th. Sponsors, Edward Schoely and Salome Laden. ("The same" here again means Father Helbron. L. F. F.).

Meclean, Margaret, of John Meclean and Rose, his wife, born March 13th, 1815, baptized by the same May 7th. Sponsors, Mosses Gelapsy and Anna Conner.

Aron, Catharine, of Joseph Aron and Margaret, his wife, born April 20th, baptized by the same May 21st. Sponsors, Henry Reinzel and Elizabeth, his wife.

Original book, page 80.

Koss, Joseph, of Joseph Koss and Mary, his wife, born April 5th, baptized by the same May 25th. Sponsors, George Reinzel and Catharine, his wife.

Borgoon, Mary Anne, of James Borgoon and Martha, his wife, born
October 30th, (evidently of the preceding year) baptized by the
same May 25th. Sponsors, Timothy Conner and Helen, his wife.

Derven, William, of Nicholas Derven and Anna, his wife, born March
16th, baptized by the same May 29th. Sponsors, Frank Kelly
and Frances, his wife.

Derven, Mary, of Nicholas Derven and Anna, his wife, born April
27th, baptized by the same May 29th. Sponsors, John Kelly and
Anna Flaningen.

(These two children apparently are of the same parents and according to the record would appear to have been born within the
same year but evidently one of the children was born in another year
and the date has not been given. L. F. F.)

Anderson, Margaret, of John Anderson and Isabel, his wife, born
August 6th, 1899 (evidently a mistake for 1809), baptized by the
same May 29th. Sponsors, John Roger and Elizabeth Flanningen.

Linch, Rose, of Bernard Linch and Wilfrida, his wife; born November 18th, baptized by the same May 29th. Sponsors, Charles
Flanningen and Mary Flanningen.

Glass, John, of Christopher Glass and Mary, his wife; date of birth
not given, baptized by the same June 2nd. Sponsors, Anthony
McMollin [McMullen?], and Mary, his daughter.

Schort, Joseph, of Frank Schort and his wife; date of birth not given,
baptized by the same June 2nd. Sponsors, Levy Borgoon and
Mary Berrny.

Gery, George, of John Gery and Catharine, his wife, born April 19th,
baptized by the same June 4th. Sponsors, George Gery and
Theresa Cread.

Septer, Joanna, of Adam Septer and Mary, his wife, born April 12th,
baptized by the same June 18th. Sponsors, John Henrich and
Mary, his wife.

Alvin, Theresa, of Jacob Alvin and Catharine, his wife, born April
20th, baptized by the same June 11th. Sponsors, Jacob Schmidt
and Susan Handall.

Meconly, John, of John Meconly and Mary, his wife, born May 10th,
baptized by the same June 11th. Sponsors, John Meclaglen and
Elizabeth Megyirsen. (Possibly McPherson).

Bell, Ruban, of John Bell and Mary his wife, born May 16th, 1813,
baptized by the same June 11th. Sponsors, Wendalin Bonn-
heimer and Catharine Morris.

Father Helbron used pages 81 & 82 for "Ordo funeralis 1800-1814.

Original book, page 83. (Two pages have been skipped and at the
head of this page 1815 is again entered).

Mecgill, Joseph, of James Mecgill and Bridget, his wife, born June 9th, baptized by the same July 9th. Sponsors, John Wagener and Barbara, his wife.

Müller, Jacob, of Martin Müller and Magdalen, his wife, born June 5th, baptized by the same August 27th. Sponsors, Joseph Henrich and Mary Kyndls.

Mecgready, John, of Patrick Mecgready and Mary, his wife, born March 8th, baptized by the same September 3rd. Sponsors, Edward Delany and Catharine Isly.

Kins, George, of Frederick Kins and Mary, his wife, born August 22nd, baptized by the same September 5th. Sponsors, Joseph Henry and Elizabeth Henrich.

(There is a memorandum here: "See page 149 where it is stated there were admitted into the Romnan Ctholic Church the following in the year 1805. March 8th, there professed the Catholic Faith, Mary Barbara Ruffner, daughter of Peter Corr and Margaret his wife. Lutherans." Then goes on the regular entry).

Aaron, Jacob, of Thomas Aaron and Susan, his wife, born February 13th, baptized by iRev. G. F. X. O'Brien, March 9th. Sponsors, Philip Cypher and Barbara Cypher.

Miller, Mary, of George Miller and Catharine, his wife, born December 6th, 1815, baptized by the same May 19th. Sponsors, John Henry and Mary Henry.

(The preceding entry is the last Baptismal entry written by Father Helbron. In Autumn 1815 he went to Philadelphia to consult a physician. On his return trip Father Helbron died at Carlisle, April 24, 1816. All entries that follow were written by Rev. G. F. X. O'Brien, pastor of St. Patrick's church, Pittsburgh. Father O'Brien attended Sportsman's Hall until Dec. 29, 1817, on which date Rev. Charles Bonaventure Maguire, who had been appointed pastor, arrived).

Stoup, Susan, of Adam Stoup and Elizabeth, his wife, born November 27th, 1815, baptized by the same May 19th. Sponsors, Peter Arisch and Mary Sendulf.

Brogan, Sarah, of Charles Brogan and Agnes, his wife, born March 1st, baptized by the same, May 19th. Sponsors, James and Catharine Haney.

Connery, Anna, of Maurice Connery and Sarah, his wife, born February 20th, baptized by the same May 19th. Sponsors, John Curran and Elizabeth McKever.

Hershman, Peter, of John Hershman and Mary, his wife, born October 18th, 1815, baptized by the same May 22nd. Sponsors, Henry Bridges and Elizabeth Bridges.

Henri, George, of James Henri and Elizabeth, his wife, born April 24th, baptized by the same May 23rd. Sponsors, John Henri and Barbara Henri.

Maracle, Solomon, of John Maracle and Barbara, his wife, born March 12th, baptized by the same May 23rd. Sponsors, Joseph Henri and Catharine Miller.

Mullen, Isabel, of Richard Mullen and Isabel, his wife, born November 27th, 1815, baptized by the same, May 23rd. Sponsors, Moses Gillespie and Bridget Rogers.

Bridges, James, of Peter Bridges and Margaret, his wife, born May 31st, baptized by the same July 14th. Sponsors, James Henry and Elizabeth Henry, his wife.

Jones, Anna, of John Jones and Elizabeth, his wife, born July 11, 1815 baptized by the same July 14th. Sponsors, Michael Curran and Catharine Clinger.

Walker, Samuel, born March 8th, baptismal ceremony supplied by the same on July 16th. Sponsors, John Harthman and Mary Harthman.

Ruffner, Margaret, of George Ruffner and Susan, his wife, born December 21st, 1815, baptismal ceremony supplied by the same, July 16th. Sponsors, Christian Sendolf and Margaret Sendolf.

Lingel, Rachel, an adult about twenty-two years of age, baptized conditionally by the same on July 17th.

Grenewalt [Grünewald?] William, of John Grenewalt and Anna, his wife, born August 15th, baptized by the same November 6th. Sponsors, Michael Curran and Sara Dougherty.

Smitt, Margaret Anna, of Joseph Smitt and Catharine, his wife, born September 5th, baptized by the same November 6th. Sponsors, Handell Bodenhamer and Margaret, his wife.

Hainy, James, born about six years ago, of Patrick Hainy and Anna, his wife, baptized by the same November 9th. Sponsor, Mary Hainy.

Hainy, Thomas, born about four years ago, of Patrick Hainy and Anna, his wife, baptized by the same November 9th. Sponsor, Catharine Hainy.

Hainy, Patrick, born about two years ago, of Patrick Hainy and Anna, his wife, baptized by the same November 9th. Sponsor, Anna Hainy.

Flower, Christian, of Valentine Flower and Margaret, his wife, born September 9th, baptized by the same November 10th. Sponsors, James and Bridget McGill.

Ruffner, Henry, of Peter Ruffner and Anna, his wife, born September 5th, baptismal ceremony supplied by the same November 10th. Sponsors, George and Mary Ruffner.

Scepter, Susan, of Adam Scepter and Mary, his wife, born April 28th, baptized by the same, November 10th. Sponsors, Peter and Margaret Bridges.

Crait, Catharine, of Daniel Crait and Sara, his wife, born October 18th, baptized by the same November 10th. Sponsors, Jacob Hainy and Elizabeth Cypher.

McLaughlin, Anna, of Michael McLaughlin and Eleanor, his wife, born March 1st, baptized by the same November 10th. Sponsors, Anthony and Isabel Dennen.

1817

Boadenhamer, Margaret, of William Boadenhamer and Mary Ann, his wife born Jan. 16th, baptized by the same February 4th. Sponsors, Handele Boadenhamer and Anna Margaret Boadenhamer. (This entry is on page 86 of the original book and is placed after seven entries which antedate it. After this entry there is a space of four inches on the page. L.F.F.)

Coon, Daniel, of Jacob Coon and Mary, his wife, born December 11, 1816, baptized by the same February 7th. Sponsors, George Coon and Mary Coon.

O'Conner, Samuel, of Dionysius O'Conner and Mary, his wife, born December 27th, 1816, baptized by the same, February 9th. Sponsors Charles Flanaghan and Catherine Flanaghan.

Noel, Daniel, of Abraham Noel and Mary, his wife, born December 3rd, 1816, baptized by the same, Februry 9th. Sponsors, Peter Noel and Margaret Noel.

McWay, Mary Ann, of Edward McWay and Anna, his wife, born November 3rd, 1816, baptized by the same, February 9th. Sponsors, James Hainy and Margery Cull.

Original book, page 86.

Crotty, Catharine, of Patrick Crotty and Anna, his wife, born December 7th, 1816, baptized by the same, February 9th. Sponsors, James Barry and Catharine Moloney.

Aaron, John, of Joseph Aaron and Margaret, his wife, born about three months ago, baptized by the same February 10th. Sponsors, Thomas Aaron and Catharine Aaron.

Miller, George, about twenty-seven years of age, baptized conditionally by the same, February 11th.

Miller, Mary Ann, of George Miller and Susan, his wife, born on the 7th of this month, baptized by the same February 12th. Sponsors, George Ruffner and Mary Ruffner.

Donnelly, Thomas, of John Donnelly and Margaret, his wife, born June 14th, 1806, baptismal ceremonies supplied by the same on April 23rd. Sponsor, James McGill.

Donnelly, James, of John Donnelly and Margaret, his wife, born December 13, 1809, ceremonies of baptism supplied by the same April 23rd. Sponsor, James Hainy.

Donnelly, Mary, of John Donnelly and Margaret, his wife, born May 2nd, 1808, ceremonies of baptism supplied by the same on April 23rd. Sponsor, Mary Hainy.

Donnelly, Isabella, of John Donnelly, and Margaret, his wife, born March 29, 1812, baptized by the same April 23rd. Sponsor, Mary McGill.

Original book, page 87.

Donnelly, Sarah, of John Donnelly and Margaret, his wife, born December 29th, 1814, baptized by the same April 23rd. Sponsor, Bridget McGill.

Coon, Mary Ann, of Adam Coon and Rachel, his wife, born March 11th, baptized by the same April 25th. Sponsors, Jacob and Mary Coon.

Flower, Daniel, of John Flower and Mary Ann, his wife, born September 9th, 1816, baptized by the same April 26th. Sponsor, Daniel Grait.

Geary, Sarah, of Martin Geary and Mary, his wife, born September 22nd, 1816, baptized by the same, April 26th. Sponsor, Sarah Grait.

Soals, Peter, of John Soals and Elizabeth, his wife, born about fourteen years ago, baptized by the same April 27th. Sponsor, Peter Noel.

Soals, Jacob, of John Soals and Elizabeth, his wife, born about twelve years ago, baptized by the same, April 27th. Sponsor, George Ruffner.

Soals, Mary, of John Soals and Elizabeth, his wife, born about sixteen years ago, baptized by the same April 27th.

Reinsel, Rachel, of George Reinsel and Catharine, his wife, born on the 14th of this month, baptized by the same April 27th. Sponsors, Adam and Rachel Coon.

O'Conner, James, of John O'Conner and Sarah, his wife, born February 4th, baptized by the same April 27th. Sponsors, John and Eleanor Layton.

Lindsay, James, of Thomas Lindsay and Sarah, his wife, born May 6th, baptized by the same August 22nd. Sponsors, George Trucks and Bridget Trucks.

Trucks, John, of George Trucks and Bridget Trucks, his wife, born May 5th, baptized by the same August 22nd. Sponsors, Barney and Mary Burgoon.

Peas, William, of James Peas and Catharine, his wife, born April 16th, baptized by the same, August 24th. Sponsors, Philip and Barbara Siford.

Coon, Elizabeth, of George Coon and Mary, his wife, born June 10th, baptized by the same August 24th. Sponsors, Jacob and Mary Coon.

Original book, page 88.

Short, Sarah, of John Short and Anna, his wife, born March 27th, baptized by the same August 24th. Sponsors, Dennis and Mary Conner.

Burgoon, Anastasia, of James Burgoon and Martha, his wife, born March 18th, baptized by the same August 24th. Sponsors, George and Mary Coon.

Geary, John, of John Geary and Catharine, his wife, born April 9th, baptized by the same August 24th. Sponsors, Conrad Reinsel and Susan Hanlin.

Peas, Mary, of James Peas and Catharine, his wife, born May 18th, 1815 baptized by the same August 24th. Sponsors, Michael Crate and Mary Siford.

Noal, Mary Ann, of Simon Noal and Mary, his wife, born June 5th, baptized by the same August 24th. Sponsors, Jacob Noal and Mary Andreis.

Glass, Mary, of Christopher Glass and Margaret, his wife, born December 12, 1815, baptized by the same, August 24th. Sponsors, John Flowers and Mary Ann Flowers.

Bridge, Matthias, of Henry Bridge and Elizabeth, his wife, born about two months ago, baptized by the same August 25th. Sponsors, George and Catharine Bridge.

Miller, Barbara, of Martin Miller and Magdalen, his wife, born August 21st of this year, baptized by Demetrius A. Gallitzin on October 14th. Sponsors, John Henry and Barbara Henry.

Original book, page 89. (At the top of this page there an entry which reads: "Order of baptisms under the administration of Father Charles Bonaventure Maguire of Ireland of the Order of St. Francis of the strict observance on the day on which I have taken possession of this benefice, namely, the 27th day of November, 1817." There is then the entry, November, 1817, standing at the head of the list. L.F.F.)

Henry, Mary Ann, of John Henry and Mary, his wife, baptized by Charles B. Maguire November 29th. Sponsors, Emmanuel Bichi [Bihi?], and Mary Zentdorf. The child was born on the 4th of December, 1817. (The 1817 was evidently meant for 1816.

75

The entry is signed "ab a Carolo B. Maguire" and some of the entries following it are signed in the same way. L.F.F.)

Coon, Mary Sibylla, of Solomon Coon and Elizabeth, his wife, born October 4th, baptized by Charles B. Maguire November 30th. Sponsors, George Ruffner and Rose Ruffner.

Miller, Catharine, of George Miller and Catharine, his wife; born November 26th, baptized by Charles B. Maguire, December 1st. Sponsors, George and Margaret Sindorf.

Original book, page 90.

Eckroth, Sarah, of Peter and Mary Eckroth, born October 19th, baptized by Charles B. Maguire December 14th. Sponsors, Joseph Henri and Sarah Miller. (The language used in these entries to record then sponsors' action is "held at the baptismal font.")

Miller, Elizabeth, of George Miller and Elizabeth, his wife, born November 18th, baptized December 14th. Sponsors, Jacob Miller and Elizabeth Eckroth.

Wilson, Margaret, a Calvinist, daughter of James Miller and Johanna, his wife, baptized December 26th. Sponsors, Edward Chevlin and Patricia Mihan.

FATHER PETER HELBRON'S GREENSBURG, PA., REGISTER

1818

Sheridan, William, of John and Catharine Sheridan, born November 30th of the preceding year, baptized January 8th. Sponsors, Patrick Lynn and Margaret Thomas.

Donnelly, William, of John and Margaret Donnelly, born August 5th, of the preceding year, baptized January 9th. Sponsor, Johanna Sheridan.

Magill, Susan, of James and Bridget Magill, born December 25th, baptized January 9th. Sponsor, Johanna Donnelly.

Donnelly, Margaret, of Henry and Johanna Donnelly, born October 20th, of the preceding year, baptized January 9th. Sponsor, Johanna Donnelly.

Original book, page 91.

[A vacant space is here left for one entry.]

Flanagan, Margaret, of Charles and Catharine Flanagan, born November 10th, baptized January 13th. Sponsors, George Coon and Mary Coon [Kuhn?]

————, Sarah, born about the middle of December, baptized January 17th. Sponsors, Henry and Elizabeth Brueck.

Kiens, Benjamin, of Frederick and Mary Kiens, born January 14th, baptized February 9th. Sponsors, Benjamin Markel and Margaret Zindorf.

Krete, Reuben, of Philip and Elizabeth Krete, born January 11th, baptized February 14th. Sponsors, Michael and Theresa Krete.

Maguire, Charles Bonaventure, of Michael and Margaret Maguire, born January 5th, baptized February 24th. Sponsors, John and Sarah O'Connor.

[Space for one entry.]

Coyle, Mary, of Philip and Catharine Coyle, born the latter part of April 1813, baptized March 15th. Sponsors, John and Cecilia Rogers.

Original book, page 92.

Ruffner, Elizabeth, of Peter and Anna Ruffner, born January 24th, baptized March 15th. Sponsors, Peter and Margaret Bridge.

McGloghlin, Sarah, of John and Susan McGloghlin, born March 13th, baptized March 20th. Sponsors, John Flower and Mary Maguire.

Shaefer, Margaret, of Henry and Mary Shaefer, born February 12th, baptized April 12th. Sponsors, Moise Gillaspy and Catharine Easley.

Aron, William, of Thomas and Susan Aron, born March 10th, baptized April 12th. Sponsors, Thomas and Catharine Aron.

Mergel, Catharine, of John and Barbara Mergel, born February 26th, baptized March 25th. Sponsors, Jacob and Mary Kuhn.

Mayer, Joseph, of Joseph and Martha Mayer, born March 6th, baptized May 10th. Sponsors, Conrad and Mary Henri.

Ruffner, Daniel, of George and Susan Ruffner, born November 10th (evidently of the preceding year) baptized May 10th. Sponsors, Jacob and Mary Kuhn.

[Space for one entry.]

Griffin, Peter, of John and Susan Griffin, born April first, baptized September 16th. Sponsors, Peter and Margaret Noel.

Original book, page 93.

Griffin, John, of John and Susan Griffin, born August 2nd, 1816, baptized September 16th. Sponsors, John and Mary Henry.

Winn, John, of John and Unity Winn, date of birth not given, baptized September 16th. Sponsors, Patrick and Margaret McGawrin.

On May 19th there were baptized at the same time Mary . . . .
[Three-fourths of a page vacant.]

Original book, page 94.

Reinsel, Catharine, of Conrad and Susan Reinsel, born July 16th, baptized August 2nd. Sponsors, Dionysius and Catharine Hanlan.

Staub, George, of Adam and Elizabeth Staub, born September 13th, baptized October 25th. Sponsors, George and Margaret Zindorf.

Berry, Margaret, of James and Anna Berry, born October 22nd, baptized October 31st. Sponsors, John Connelly and Margaret McFee.

O'Connor, Charles Bonaventure, of Dionysius and Mary O'Connor, born September 21st, baptized November 1st. Sponsors, Henry Reinsel and Anna O'Connor.

Maguire, George, of Johanna Maguire, born December 15th, 1816, baptized November 29th. Sponsors, James and Neremia Maguire.

Maglin, John, of John and Rose Maglin, born January 15th, 1817, baptized November 29th. Sponsor, Bernard McManus.

Maglin, Edward, of John and Rose Maglin, born August 15th, baptized November 29th. Sponsor, John O'Connor.

Toner, Mary, of Matthew and Anna Toner, born December 13th, baptized December 13th. Sponsors, Michael O'Kelly and Anna Dogharty.

1819

Laden, James, of John and Eleanor Laden, born December 20th, baptized January 31st. Sponsors, John and Elizabeth O'Connor.

Eckroth, Martha, of John and Catharine Eckroth, born December 14th, (evidently of the preceding year) baptized January 31st. Sponsors, Christian Bock and Sarah Miller.

O'Connor, Eleanor, of John and Sarah O'Connor, born on the 25th of this month, baptized February 28th. Sponsors, John and Mary Laden.

Miller, Sarah Anna, of Peter and Elizabeth Miller, born February 16th, baptized March 7th. Sponsors, Peter and Mary Eckroth.

McVey, William, of Edward and Anna McVey, born January 23rd, baptized April 10th. Sponsors, Peter and Bridget Rodgers.

Aron, Thomas, of Daniel and Mary Aron, born April 2nd, baptized April 22nd. Sponsors, Thomas and Catharine Aron.

Stephani, Aloysius, of Aloysius and Neoburga Stephani, born March 1st, 1818, baptized April 25th. Sponsors, David Gildner and Eva Zindorf.

Coon [Kuhn?] Catharine Anna, of Jacob and Mary Coon, born March 25th, baptized April 25th. Sponsors, Caspar Easley and Catharine Rufner.

Aron, Mary Margaret, of Joseph and Margaret Aron, born December 29th, 1818, baptized April 25th. Sponsors, Thomas and Susan Aron.

Burgoon, Bridget, of Barnabas and Mary Burgoon, born December 25, 1818, baptized April 25th. Sponsors James and Mary MaGuff.

Scepter, Juliana, of Adam and Mary Scepter, born October 26th (evidently of the preceding year), baptized May 30th. Sponsors, Joseph and Margaret Noel.

Merigel, Mary Theresa, of John and Barbara Merigel, born April 12th. baptized May 30th. Sponsors, John and Mary Henry.

Flour, Elizabeth, of Valentine and Margaret Flour, born April 17th, baptized June 6th. Sponsors, Henry and Elizabeth Reinsel.

Kiens, Rose, of Frederick and Mary Kiens, born May 14th, baptized June 6th. Sponsors, Joseph and Theresa Henry.

Wade, Rose, of George and Elizabeth Wade, born April 30th, baptized June 6th. Sponsors, Henry Bock and Susan Noel.

Brogan, Rose, of Charles and Agnes Brogan, born May 16th, baptized June 6th. Sponsors, Henry and Johanna Donnelly.

Ruffner, Sarah, of Peter and Anna Ruffner, born April 18th, baptized June 13th. Sponsors, Simon and Christina Ruffner.

Ruffner, Mary Anna, of Peter and Anna Ruffner, born April 18th, baptized June 13th. Sponsors, Jacob and Mary Coon.

Krete, Daniel, of Daniel and Sarah Krete, born May 28th, baptized June 20th. Sponsors, John and Catharine Geary.

Smith, John, of Joseph and Catharine Smith, born June 5th, baptized July 4th. Sponsors, John and Mary Rogers.

Original book, page 97.

Burgoon, Theresa, of James and Martha Burgoon, born June 16th, baptized July 4th. Sponsors, James Magill and Catharine Maguire.

Ruffner, Valentine, of George and Rose Ruffner, born July 9th, baptized July 15th. Sponsors, Valentine Reinsel and Rose Buck.

O'Kelly, Dionysius, of John and Alice O'Kelly, born February 26th, 1818, baptized August 22nd. Sponsors, Edward Shovlin and Catharine Maguire.

Miller, Catharine, of Martin and Magdalen Miller, born July 11th, baptized August 29th. Sponsors, Conrad and Mary Henry.

Reed, Mary, of Meredith and Eleanor Reed, born August 30th, baptized October 10th. Sponsors, James and Catharine Heaney.

Shaeffer, Ludovic, of Henry and Mary Schaeffer, born September 18th, baptized October 24th. Sponsors, Ferdinand and Margaret Easley.

Dotzin, Samuel, of William and Elizabeth Dotzin, born on the 7th of this month, baptized in July. (Date of baptism not given). Sponsors, John and Anna Short.

McMullin, Elizabeth, of Enis and Catharine McMullin, born January 13, 1818, baptized in the month of July (date of baptism not given.) Sponsors, George Trucks and Anna Maguire.

Trucks, George, of George and Bridget Trucks, born March 9th, baptized in the month of July (date not given). Sponsors, Thomas Maguff and Eleanor Maguire.

Henry, John, of Conrad and Mary Henry, born August 28th, baptized in the month of September (date of baptism not given). Sponsors, John and Mary Henry.

Original book, page 98.

Reinsel, Mary, of Conrad and Susan Reinsel, born September 30th, baptized October 30th. Sponsors, Henry and Catharine Coon.

Short, Samuel, of John and Anna Short, born August 20th, baptized November 14th. Sponsors, Michael and Margaret Maguire.

Noel, John, of Joseph and Margaret Noel, born November 26th, 1811 baptized November 14th. Sponsors, Edward and Mary Toner.

Regan, Matthew, of John and Mary Regan, born October 23rd, 1818, baptized November 21st. Sponsors, John Connelly and Margaret Mongomery.

———, John, born 20th of this month, baptized November 22nd. Sponsors, David Mulhollin and Mary Eckroth.

Noel, Sarah, of Simon, and Mary Noel, born October 19th, baptized November 28th. Sponsors, Joseph Bock and Sarah Dogherty.

Sceptre, Simon, born November 25th, 1810, Margaret, born November 6th, 1812, and David, born January 28th, 1815, of Frederick and Catharine Sceptre, baptized November 28th. Sponsors, Frederick Sceptre and Margaret Noel.

Harkins, Bridget, of Daniel and Margaret Harkins, born on the 9th of this month, baptized December 11th. Sponsors, James Doyle and Bridget McKrey.

Diamond, Silas, of Philip and Sarah Diamond, born November 3rd, baptized December 19th. Sponsors, James Heaney and Sophy Burk.

Original book, page 99.

Shannon, Edward, of John and Mary Shannon, born 17th of this month, baptized December 24th. Sponsors, Patrick Shannon and Margaret McFee.

Aron, Mary, wife of Conrad Aron, converted from heresy, baptized December 26th. Sponsors, Thomas and Susan Aron.

Aron, Anna, of Conrad and Mary Aron, born November 23rd, baptized December 26th. Sponsors, John Klinger and Elizabeth Seifert.

1820.

Rogers, John, of John and Cecilia Rogers, born December 19th, baptized January 30th. Sponsors, James and Mary Rogers.

Rogers, Mary, of Nicholas and Eleanor Rogers, born December 20th (evidently of the preceding year) baptized January 30th. Sponsors, Maurice and Anna McBride.

Coon [Kuhn?] Rose, of Adam and Regina Coon, born June 9th, 1819, baptized January 30th. Sponsors, Peter and Margaret Bridge.

Henry, Mary Barbara, of Joseph and Theresa Henry, born January 3rd, baptized February 22nd. Sponsors, John and Barbara Henry.

Ziegler, Elizabeth, of Jacob and Catharine Ziegler, born February 18th, baptized February 22nd. Sponsor, Magdalen Noel.

Noel, Mary Barbara, of Abraham and Magdalen Noel, born January 30th, baptized February 22nd. Sponsor, Barbara Ruffner.

Original book, page 100.

Miller, George, of George and Elizabeth Miller, born February 25th, baptized March 26th. Sponsors, Nicholas and Anna Miller.

Heaney, Elizabeth, of Patrick and Anna Heaney, born January 26th, baptized March 26th. Sponsors, Henry Reinsel and Mary MaGill.

Mayer, Christian, of Joseph and Martha Mayer, born November 5th, 1819, baptized April 2nd. Sponsors, John and Barbara Henry.

Maguire, Philip, of Prendergast and Sarah Maguire, born February 20th, baptized April 3rd. Sponsors, Christian Buck and Anna Miller.

Aron, Thomas, of Thomas and Susan Aron, born the 11th of this month, baptized April 30th. Sponsors, George Aron and Elizabeth Seifert.

81

Cantwell, Albert, of James and Susan Cantwell, born the 24th of this month, baptized May 28th. Sponsors, Andrew and Eleanor Maguire.

O'Connor, Catharine, of Dionysius and Mary O'Connor, born April 5th, baptized May 28th. Sponsors, Thomas Shannon and Elizabeth O'Connor.

Crete, Theresa, of Philip and Elizabeth Crete, born February 25th, baptized May 28th. Sponsors, James Heaney and Theresa Crete.

Original book, page 101.

Geary, Magdalen, of John and Catharine Geary, born February 22nd, baptized May 28th. Sponsors, Daniel and Sarah Crete.

Campbell, Isabel, wife of John Campbell, converted from Calvinism, baptized May 28th. Sponsors, Edward Toner and Catharine Maguire.

Johnson, James, of Thomas and Anna Johnson, born April 20th, baptized May 28th. Sponsors, Connell and Catharine Johnson.

Johnson, Charles, of Connell and Catharine Johnson, born February 1st, baptized February 1st. Sponsors, Edward and Unity Shovlin.

Lempen, Mary, of John and Margaret Lempen, six years old, baptized June 1st. Sponsors, John and Margaret Henry.

———, Mary Sidney, born March 12th, baptized June 1st. Sponsors, Nicholas and Sarah Miller.

Henry, Elizabeth, of Conrad and Mary Henry, born June 23rd, baptized July 30th. Sponsors, Frederick and Mary Kiens.

O'Connor, Anna, of John and Sarah O'Connor, born July 2nd, baptized July 30th. Sponsors, Michael and Margaret Maguire.

Original book, page 102.

Donnelly, Isabel, of Henry and Johanna Donnelly, born on the 6th of this month, baptized July 30th. Sponsors, Edward Toner and Margaret Donnelly.

Staub, John Christian, of Adam and Elizabeth Staub, born June 28th, baptized July 30th. Sponsors, Peter and Eva Zindorf.

Murry, Rebecca, of Daniel and Rebecca Murry, born December 25th, 1819, baptized July 30th. Sponsors, Dionysius and Mary O'Connor.

Barry, John, of James and Anna Barry, born July 19th, baptized July 30th. Sponsors, John Harkins and Anna Ferry.

Mullin, Eleanor, of Richard and Isabel Mullin, born July 4th, baptized July 30th. Sponsors, Meredith Toner and Catharine Rodgers.

Eastley, Andrew Jacob, of Caspar and Rachel Eastley, born September 23rd, baptized December 9th. Sponsors, James and Martha Eastley.

Aron, John, of Daniel and Mary Aron, born October 5th, baptized December 9th. Sponsors, George Aron and Margaret Rufner.

Rufner, Henry, of George and Rose Rufner, born November 5th, baptized December 9th. Sponsors, John and Catharine Bock.

Coon [Kuhn?] Mary Matilda, of Solomon and Elizabeth Coon, born September 1st, baptized December 9th. Sponsors, Jacob and Mary Coon.

Original book, page 103.

Mohn, Francis, of Hugo and Eleanor Mohn, born November 17th, baptized December 10th. Sponsors, Walter and Sarah O'Hanlan.

(Note: In the original book of entry, on page 149 are the following entries).

Margaret Wilson, daughter of James and Johanna Wilson has professed the Catholic Faith in the presence of Edward Chevlin and and Patrick Mihan as witnesses, second of January, 1818.

Jacob Barket, a Lutheran, has professed the Catholic Faith in the presence of John and Mary Henry on the 23rd of April, 1819.

John Lamping, has professed the Catholic Faith in the presence of Conrad Henry and David Mulhollin, 27th February 1820.

Original book, page 119.

(No date) James McCaddin, forty-seven years old, in a public profession renounced the Lutheran heresy and was baptized conditionally.

Margaret Donnelly, aged forty-two years, in a public profession renounced the Calvinistic heresy and was conditionally baptized. The witnesses were John Donnelly and Michael Maguire.

1821

Original book, page 103.

Cornin, Margaret, of Charles and Susan Cornin, born near Youngstown in this State on the second day of this month, baptized March 8th by Rev. T. McGirr on March 11th. Sponsors, Doctor McGirr and Eleanor McGirr.

[Note: In this and the following entries the sponsors are said to have held the child—" suspnt."]

Miller, John, of Peter and Elizabeth Miller, born on the 11th day of February of this year in the town called Unity, baptized by the Rev. Terence McGirr on March the 11th. Sponsors, George and Susan Miller.

Coon, [Kuhn?] Jacob, of George and Mary Coon, born in a place called Hempfield, in this State, on the 28th day of December 1820, baptized by the same on March 11th. Sponsors, Dionysius Conner and Margaret Eastly.

Reinsel, John, of Conrad and Susan Reinsel, born in a place called Derry Township on the 28th day of January of this year, baptized by the same on March 25th. Sponsors, Anthony Reinsel and Elizabeth Hanlin.

Kerrigan, John, of Mordecai and Mary Kerrigan, born in the town called Derry towship on the 17th day of February of this year, baptized by the same on March 25th. Sponsors, John and Mary Keregan.

Leadin, Mary Ann, of John and Eleanor Leadin, born at Unity on the 20th day of March of this year, baptized by the same April (date not given). Sponsors, Philip McBride and Mary Leadin.

Sloey, Margaret, of Hugo and Mary Sloey, born near the town called Youngstown in this State in the Month of March of this year, baptized by the same on April 20th. Sponsor, Matilda Coll.

Hearkins, Unity, of Hugo and Isabel Hearkins, born on the 12th of April, 1820, baptized by the same on April 23rd. Sponsor, Rachel Coon.

Henry, George, of Adam and Rachel Henry, born on the 24th day of March, 1821, baptized by the same on April 22nd. Sponsors, Henry Rensel and Margaret Ruffener.

Myer, Elizabeth, of Joseph and Martha Myer, born on the 28th day of March, 1821, baptized by the same on April 22nd. Sponsors, Joseph Akerman and Elizabeth Hanlin.

Lampin, John, of John and Margaret Lampin, born in this State on the 12th of November, 1820, baptized by the same on April 26th. No sponsors given.

Original book, page 104.

Johnson, John, of Thomas and Anna Johnson, born in the town called Unity, on the 14th day of this month and year, baptized by the same on April 27th. Sponsors, Edward and his wife Anna Shevlin.

Diamond, Margaret, of William and Esther Diamond, born in the town called Derry township on the 11th day of January of this year, baptized by the same May 31st. Sponsors, John and his wife Anna Short.

[Space for one entry.]

Ruffener, Isaac, of George and Susan Ruffener, born on the 21st day of July, 1820, baptized by the same May 10th. Sponsors, George and Mary Ruffener.

Scuptre, Jacob, of Frederick and Catharine Scuptre, born on the 10th of December 1820, baptized by the same May 10th. Sponsors, Jacob Noel and Margaret Senduff.

Orange, John Henry, of Peter and Margaret Orange, born 27th of August, 1820, baptized by the same May 10th. Sponsors, Daniel and Sarah Crete.

Nesler, Michael, of Blosius and Rose Nesler, born 27th of September 1820, baptized by the same on May 11th. Sponsors, Michael Crete and Margaret Ruffener.

84

Stephan, John Godfrey, of Ludovic and Prudentia Stephan, born August 16th, 1820, baptized by the same on May 11th. Sponsors, Henry Bridge and Mary Kelly.

McLaughlin, Susan, of John and Susan McLaughlin, born on the 10th of March of this year, baptized by the same May 11th. Sponsors, Richard and Susan Hare.

Original book, page 105.

Kentz, John, of Frederick and Mary Kentz, born in the town called Unity on the 28th day of June, baptized by the same August 10th. Sponsors, John Henry and his wife Margaret.

Miller, Mary Elizabeth, of Martin and McLena Miller, born near Hannatown on the 28th day of June of this year, baptized by the same on August 12th. Sponsors, Joseph and his wife Theresa Miller.

Hearkins, Hugo, nearly 16 years old, of John and Elizabeth Hearkins, baptized August 12. Sponsor James McGill.

Hearkins, of John and Elizabeth Hearkins, nine years, making it the 18th day of March, 1811, baptized by the same August 15th. Sponsor, Christian Ruffener.

Miller, Sarah, of George and Susan Miller, born on the 27th day of July of this year, baptized by the same on August 15th. No sponsors given.

Hearkins, Margaret, of John and Elizabeth Hearkins, born on the 18th of July of this year, baptized by the same on August 15th. Sponsors, Jacob Coon and Catharine Eastly.

Burk, John, of William and Johanna Burk, born on the 5th of July in Derry township, baptized by the same on September 23rd. Sponsors, Edward and his daughter Anna Toner.

Septer, Joseph, of Henry and Elizabeth Septer, born on the first of October, 1820, baptized by the same on September 23rd. Sponsors, Bernard Grant and Maggy Coll.

Septer, Frank, of Adam and Mary Septer, born on the 16th of November, 1821, baptized on September 23rd. Sponsors, Henry Buck and Catharine Rodgers.

[Note: There is evidently an error here either in the date of birth or in the date of baptism. As there are no entries for November and December, it is quite possible that the date of baptism is wrong.]

Reed, John, of Mordecai and Eleanor Reed, born on the 18th day of this month and year and baptized on September 28th. Sponsors, Bernard McGirr and Rose Kienan.

Original book, page 106.

Shiffer, Ferdinand, of Henry and Mary Shiffer, born on the 17th of September of this year and baptized by the same on September 28th. Sponsors, Christopher Ruffner and Catharine Eastley.

November, by the same.

[Vacant space for entry.]

85

Buck, Sarah, of John and Catharine Buck, born on the 11th of January of this year, baptized by the same on February 6th. Sponsors, George and Susan Miller.

Glepsy, Lucilda, of James and Elizabeth Glepsy, born in Derry township on the 9th of May of this year, baptized by the same June 7th. Sponsors, Con. Johnston and Rose McKenna.

Aron, Jacob, of Conrad and Mary Aron, born on the 4th of May of this year, baptized by the same on June 16th. Sponsors, Solomon Sippert and Elizabeth Aron.

Conor, Mary, of John and Sarah Conor, born on the 27th of May of this year, baptized by the same on June 16th. Sponsors, Bernard McGirr and Anna Leadin.

Geary, Joseph, of John and Catharine Geary, born on the 9th of February of this year, baptized by the same on June 23rd. Sponsors, John and his wife Elizabeth Crete.

Original book, page 143.

" See the end of this volume, page 99 (143)." The following five baptisms are entered on page 99 (143) A. D. 1822.

Crete, Elizabeth, of Daniel and Sarah Crete, born on the 11th of December, 1821, baptized by Rev. T. McGirr on April 19th. Sponsors, Michael Crete and Elizabeth Cipphers.

Crete, Elizabeth, of Philip and Elizabeth Crete, born on the 9th of April of this year, baptized by the same May 12th. Sponsors, Daniel and his wife Sarah Crete.

Peters, Anna Mary, about six years old, born of non-Catholic parents, baptized by the same on May 12th. Sponsors, Henry and his wife Catharine Coon.

Conor, Margaret Lusilda, of Dionysius and Mary Conor, born on the 8th of this month and year, baptized May 17th. Sponsors, John and his wife Sarah Conor.

Cassidy, Bridget, of Patrick and Bridget Cassidy, born on the 29th, of January of this year, baptized by the same on May 26th. Sponsors, Hugh Conway and Margaret McGill.

Original book, page 107.

Johnson, Edward, of Constantine and Catharine Johnson, born at Derry township on the 17th day of this year, baptized by the same on July 17th. Sponsors, Dionysius Conor and his wife.

Fitzsummens, William, of Patrick and Elizabeth Fitzsummens, born on the 3rd of April of this year, baptized by the same on August 3rd. Sponsors, John Poynta and Gena Leadin.

Tolin, William, of Jeremiah and Mary Tolin, born on the 1st of April of this year, baptized by the same on August 3rd. Sponsors, Frederick Kintz and Margaret Sendoff.

Rodgers, Eleanor, of John and Cecilia Rogers, born on the 27th of July, of this year, baptized by the same on August 11th. Sponsors, Edward Toner and Ally Mullen.

Stoup, Mary Ann, of Adam and Elizabeth Stoup, born on the 28th of of May of this year, baptized by the same August 11th. Sponsors, George and his wife Elizabeth Topper.

McFee, John, of John and Catharine McFee, born on the 2nd of August of this year, baptized September (date not given). Sponsors, Felix McBride and Anna Henry.

Eastly, John, of Caspar and Rachel Eastly, born on the 9th of August of this year, baptized by the same September 1st. Sponsors, Jacob and his wife Mary Coon.

Original book, page 108.

Buck, Henry, of Joseph and Elizabeth Buck, born on the 17th of August, baptized by the same September 8th. Sponsors, Christopher Buck and Mary Hanlin.

Keys, John, of Joseph and Mary Keys, born on the 7th of July of this year, baptized by the same September 8th. Sponsors, George Coon and his wife Mary.

Barr, James, of Daniel and Mary Barr, born on the 1st of this month, and year, baptized by the same on the 17th of September. Sponsors, Cornelius Campbell and Sarah Henry.

Rensel, Joseph, of Anthony and Elizabeth Rensel, born on the 22nd of September of this year, baptized by the same on October 3rd. Sponsors, Dionysius and his wife Catharine Rensel.

McMullen, William, of John and Mary McMullen, born on the 9th day of the month of September of this year, baptized by the same on October 13th. Sponsors, John Toner and Catharine Eastly.

McGinn, Margaret Anastasia, of John P. and Martha McGinn, born on the 28th of September of this year, baptized by the same on October 21st. Sponsor, Eleanor McGirr.

Meehan, James, of Roger H. Meehan, born on the 4th of this month and year, baptized by the same on November 10th. Sponsors, Patrick and his wife R. McDermott.

McGuire, Rose, of Prendergast and Sarah McGuire, born on the 1st of October of this year, baptized by the same December 18th. Sponsors, Barnabas Shirly and Catharine McQuire.

Original book, page 109.

[December 20th, space for one entry.]

FATHER PETER HELBRON'S GREENSBURG, PA., REGISTER

Copied from the original by the Rev. Father John, O. S. B. Translated by Lawrence F. Flick, M.D., LL.D.

As will be noticed, this final installment of the Greensburg Register contains not only the Records of the Baptisms, but also the Marriage and Burial Records, together with a list of the number of Easter confessions heard by Father Helbron in the years 1801-1815.

Johnson, William, of Thomas and Anna Johnson, born on the 13th of this month and year, baptized on February 27th by Rev. Terrence McGirr. Sponsors, Michael and his wife Anna Kelly.

Coon, Susan Catherine, of Solomon and Elizabeth Coon, born on 29th day of January of this year, baptized by the same on March 22d. Sponsors, Henry and his wife Catherine Coon.

Hearkins, Charles Rodgers, of John and Bridget Hearkins, born on 19th of October 1822, baptized by the same on March 22d. Sponsors, John and Bridget Rodgers.

Aron, Philip Ciphert, of Daniel and Mary Magdalen Aron, born on 23d day of February of this year, baptized by the same March 31st. Sponsors, Patrick Donaghy and Eleanor McGirr.

[Space for 2 entries.]

Original book, page 110.

Campbell, James, of John and Isabella Campbell, born at Greensburg of the 8th of the May of this year, baptized by Rev. T. McGirr on June 15th. Sponsors, Cornelius Campbell and Eleanor Cain.

Rey, Susan of John and Catharine Rey, born at Derry on the 25th of April, A. D. 1822, baptized by the same on June 15th. Sponsors, Bernard Shery and Mary McGill.

Kelly, John Miracle, of John and Margaret Kelly born on the 6th day of this month and year, baptized by the same on June 11th. Sponsor, Miss Kelly.

[Space 2-3 page, room for 5 entries.]

Original book, page 111.

Rodgers, Bridget of Cornelius and Eleanor Rodgers, born on the 2d of February of this year, baptized by the same June 29th. Sponsors, Henry Montgomery and Sarah O'Donell.

Buck, Henry of John and Catherine Buck, born on the 3rd of this month and in this year, baptized by the same on June 29th. Sponsors, George and Mary Ruffener.

Kintz, Elizabeth of Frederick and Mary Kintz, born on the 24th of July of this year, baptized by the same on August 10th. Sponsors, John and his wife Elizabeth Kintz.

Coon, Jacob of George and Mary Coon, born on the 8th of August of this year, baptized by the same on August 31st. Sponsors, Henry and his wife Catherine. (Family name not given.)

Nesler, Elizabeth of Blasius and Rose Nesler, born on the 19th of June of this year, baptized by the same on November 2d. (No sponsors given.)

Stephan, Henry of Louis and Bana Stephan, born on the 13th of June of this year, baptized by the same on November 2d. (No sponsors given.)

Skelly, John Henry, of Hugo and Mary Skelly, born on the 8th of October of this year, (Nothing further said about when baptized, probably November 2d.) Sponsors, Wm. Eastly and Eleanor Brown.

Original book, page 112. [Space 1¼ pages for 12 entries.]

1824.

Original book, page 113.

Leadin, John, of John and Eleanor Leadin, born on 24th of November A. D. 1823, baptized by Rev. Terrence McGirr, February 8th. Sponsors, Bernard McGirr and Mary McDermott.

Coon, Susan, of Jacob and Mary Coon, born February 19th of this year, baptized by the same March 25. Sponsors, George and Catherine Rensel.

Rensel, Anthony, of George and Catherine Rensel, born on the 21st of February of this year, baptized by the same on March 25th. Sponsors, Jacob and Mary Coon.

Eckrod, Mary, of John and Catherine Eckrod, born on the 25th of June A. D. 1821, baptized, by the same March 25th. Sponsor, Barbara Miracle.

Eckrod, Jacob, of John and Catherine Eckrod, born on the 3d of November A. D. 1822, baptized by the same on March 25. Sponsors, Christopher Buck and Mary Kintz.

Eckrod, Peter, of John and Catherine Eckrod, born on the 12th of April A. D. 1823, baptized by the same March 25th. Sponsors, Joseph and Rose Buck.

[Space for one entry.]

Tolen, Michael, of Jeremiah and Mary Tolen, born on the first of March of this year, baptized by the same on April 11th. Sponsors, Michael O'Brien and Anna Kelly.

Reed, Catherine of Matthew and Bridget Reed, born on the 14th of
May of this year, baptized by the same on April 11th. Sponsors,
Bernard McGirr and Catherine Boner.

[Space for one entry.]

Original book, page 114.

Keenan, James, of James and Isabella Keenan, born at Youngstown,
17th of September, A. D. 1823, baptized by Rev. T. McGirr on
September 28th. Sponsors, Hugo and Rose Keenan.

Henry, Conrad James, of Conrad and Mary Henry, born on 28th of
November, A. D. 1824, in Unity Township, baptized by the same
December 12th. Sponsors, John and Elizabeth Kintz.

1825.

Grünwalt, Mary, of John and Anna Grünwalt, born in this town called
Unity on the 14th of February of this year and baptized by the
same on March 14th. Sponsors, William and his wife Margaret
Dougherty.

Kelly, Joseph, of Patrick and Margaret Kelly, born in the the same town
on the 17th of this month of this year, baptized by the same on
March 22nd. Sponsor, Margaret Kelly.

Cassidy, Anna of Patrick and Bridget Cassidy, born on the 3rd of
November A. D. 1824, baptized by the same on April 3rd. Sponsors, Caspar Tar, Magistrate and Mary Henry.

Sendoff, George, of Christopher and Margaret Sendoff, born on the
4th of January of this year, baptized by the same on April 3rd.
Sponsors, John Henry and Mary Sendoff.

Original book, page 115.

Kintz, Elizabeth Catherine, of Frederic and Mary Kintz, born on the
9th of April of this year, baptized by the same on May 1st. Sponsors, John Markle and Elizabeth Kintz.

Leonard, Anna, of John and A, Leonard, born on the 21st of September
A. D. 1824, baptized by the same on May 1st. Sponsors, John
McMullen and Eleanor McGirr.

Miller, Nicholas, of George and Elizabeth Miller, born on the 13th of
March of this year, baptized by the same on May 15th. Sponsors,
Henry Sendoff and Mary Kintz.

Coon, William Jacob of Solomon and Elizabeth Coon, born on the
4th of September of this year, baptized by the same on October 23rd.
Sponsors, Peter Toner and Catherine Ruffener.

Coon, Leo, of George and Mary Coon, born on the 14th of September
of this year, baptized by the same October 23rd. Sponsors, Joseph
Smith and his wife.

Boner, Sarah, of Patrick and Sarah Boner, born on the 16th of January of this year, baptized by the same on February 12th. Sponsors, Michael McKernan and Jeana Brogan.

Ruffener, William, of Simon and Jeana Ruffener, born on the 19th of January of this year, baptized by the same February 21st. Sponsors, James Leaden and Susan Miller.

Davis, Elizabeth of Robert and Bridget Davis, born on the 6th of August of this year, baptized by the same in 1826 (exact date not given.) Sponsors, John McMullin and Margaret Curry.

1827.

Original book, page 116.

Johnson, Bridget, of Thomas and Anna Johnson, born on the 31st of December 1826, baptized by Rev. Ter. McGirr (date of baptism not given.) Sponsors, John Gallagher and Anna Duff.

Coon, Cornelius, of Adam and Rachel Coon, born on the 24th of May in this town called Unity, baptized by the same September 1st. Sponsors, Frank Kelly and Catherine Flanagan.

McBride, John, of Philip and Mary McBride, born on the 26th of August of this year in this town, baptized by the same September 2nd. Sponsors, Edward Shevelin and Anna Kintz.

[Rest of page vacant.]

Original book, page 117.

1828.

Coon, Mary Magdalen, of George and Mary Coon, born in this town on the 29th of November A. D. 1827 (date of baptism not given.) Sponsors, Martin and his wife Martha Miller.

[Rest of page vacant.]

Original book, page 118.

January 22nd, 1829. Nothing else, no entries for the year. Among the marriage entries Rev. Ter. McGirr entered the following baptisms for the year 1828.

Original book, page 136.

Stephan, Catherine, of Ludovic and Burga Stephen, born on the 4th of June A. D. 1824 near Greensburg, baptized by the same May 29th. Sponsors, Andrew Crete and Catherine Hergan.

Rukey, Mary Ann, of John and Catherine Rukey, born on the 19th of February A. D. 1824 at Greensburg, baptized by the same May 29th. Sponsors, Andrew Hogen and Amelia Mack.

91

McBride, Mary, of Philip and Mary McBride, born and baptized by the same on the same day in this town, May 21st. Sponsors, James McBride and Eleanor McBride.

Original book, page 121.

1800.

Gallegar-Meckuy: May 10, 1800, in the Church, John Gallegar to Margaret Meckuy. Peter Helbron, pastor.

1801.

Car-Boyl. November 10, 1801, Patrick Car to Petronilla Boyl. Peter Helbron pastor.

1802.

Devine-Meily: January 19, 1802, Michael Devine born in Ireland to Margaret Meily, non-Catholic, unmarried.

Brick-Ruffner: June 1, 1802, Peter Brick to Margaret Ruffner.

Beyl-Graeffert: June 5, 1802, Michael Beyl to Schiny Graeffert from Theron township.

Original book, page 122.

Keller-Meccferly: November 8, 1802, Anthony Keller to Margaret Meccferly, widow.

........-McQuire: November 9, 1802, John ...., baptized before marriage, to Anna McQuire daughter of John McQuire.

Müller-Henry: May 30, 1803, after the customary banns had been announced by me the undersigned, they were solemnly united in matrimony, Martin Müller to Magdalen Henry. Peter Helbron, pastor.

Lees-Reys: August 1, 1803 in the Church John Lees, born in Ireland to Easter Reys, born in America.

O'Dannell-Rogers: August 16, in the Church, Daniel O'Dannell and Cecilia Rogers.

1804.

Brannen-Connor: January 2, 1804 in the Church, Michael Brannen to Mary Connor.

Original book, page 123.

Wickly-Ruffner. February 7, 1804 in the Church, William Wickly to Barbara Ruffner.

Meckbraid-Meckyu: April 9, 1804, Neal Meckbraid to Sibbila Meckyu.

Ruffner-Grünewald: July 1, 1804, George Ruffner to Elizabeth Grünewald, daughter of John Grünewald.

Bitcher-Gilaspy: September —, 1804, Feilman Bitcher from New England to Susan Gilaspy.

1805.

Hillenee-Braun: .... 1805 Athorus Hillenee from Ireland to Mary Braun. Both from Washington.

Mecdavid-Lachery: January 12, 1805, Patrick Mecdavid to Helen Lachery.

1806.

Darboy-Arnold: April 6, 1806, Lawrence Darboy to Honora Arnold.

Original book, page 124.

Hendel-Brauer: April 13, Joseph Hendel to Mary Brauer.

1807.

Meccgynly-Calegarh: May 18, James Meccgynly son of James and Bridget Meccgynly to Catherine Calegar daughter of Adam and Mary Calegar, before witness. (names of witness not given).

Schams-Schearer: July 12, 1807, Edward Victor Schams to Mary Schearer.

Reys-Mittneight: July 13, 1807, John Reys to Genieve Mittneight.

[Note: The two preceding entries are recorded in somewhat different form, the phrases " on the one part " and " on the other part " being used. They were entered by Father Helbron.

1808.

Kins-Henrich: August 16, 1808, Frederick Kins to Mary Henrich. Peter Helbron, Pastor.

Original book, page 125.

Ruffner-Zinsdorff: November 15, 1808, George Adam Ruffner to Susan Elizabeth Zinsdorff. [Note: Although this entry reads " Before me the undersigned" there is no signature.—L. F. F.

Harcken-Harken: November 20, 1808, Neail Harcken to Bridget Harken.

1809.

Reinzell-Dapper: January 3, 1809, Henry Reinzell to Elizabeth Dapper.

Conner-Kuhn: April 25, 1809, Dionysius Conner to Margaret Kuhn.

Kuhn-Faust: April 25, 1809, Henry Kuhn to Catherine Faust.

Mequeyer-Conner: May 12, 1909, Michael Mequeyer to Margaret Conner.

Schmidt-Peals: June 6, 1809, Jacob Schmidt to Catherin Peals.

Original book, page 126.

Kuhn-Ruffner: July 10, 1809, Jacob Kuhn to Mary Ruffner.

1810.

Henrick-Zinsdorff: May 8, 1810, John Henrick to Mary Zinsdorff.

[Here there is an entry of a death which reads as follows: August 4, having been provided with all the Sacraments, Matthias Wagner died aged 84 years.]

Brotice-Ruffner: October 30, 1810, John Brotice to Anna Ruffner. John Brotice returning to Clearfield with his spouse.

1811.

Bicks-Seyvert: May 7, 1811, James Bicks, Calvinist, to Catherine Seyvert, Catholic, the husband promising that the children born would be baptized and brought up in the Catholic Religion.

1812.

Trox-Megough: ...... 26, 1812, George Trox to Bridget Megough.

Reinzel-Dapper: July 7, 1812, Gregory Reinzel to Catherine Dapper.

Original book, page 127.

Muller-Zinsdorff: July 7, 1812, Gregory Muller to Catherine Zinsdorff.

Noel-Andressin: August 12, 1812, Simon Noell to Mary Andressin.

1813.

Muller-Gelaspy: ...... 2, 1813, Jacob Muller to Johanna Gelaspy, both from Brownsville.

Aron-Dapper: February 16, 1812, Joseph Aron to Margaret Dapper.

Gerry-Bauman. February 23, 1813, John Gerry to Catherine Bauman.

1815.

Müller-Ruffner: May 4, 1815, George Müller to Susan Ruffner.

Arron-Seyfert: May 9, 1815, Thomas Arron to Susan Seyfert.

Original book, page 128.

May 15: Marriages contracted before a magistrate were renewed by me after offspring of heretical marriage according to the rites of the Church. [No names of such parties were entered. L. F. F.]

Henry-Brick: July 4, 1815, James Henry to Elizabeth Brick.

Laden-O'Conner: July 4, 1815, John Laden to Petronilla O'Conner.

Flanningen-Kuhn: September 12, 1815, Charles Flanningen to Catherine Kuhn.

1816.

O'Conner-Layton: May 21, 1816, John O'Connor to Sarah Layton. G. F. X. O' Brien.

Schaffer-Easley: November 10, 1816, Henry Schaffer to Mary Easley. G. F. X. O'Brien.

94

Henry-Keans: April 27, 1817, Conrad Henry to Mary Keans. G. F. X. O'Brien.

McLaughlin-McGuire. April 28, 1817, John McLaughlin to Susan McGuire. G. F. X. O'Brien.

Reinsel-Hanlin: August 26, 1817, Conrad Reinsel to Susan Hanlin. G. F. X. O'Brien.

Lynch-Wilson: December .., 1817, James Lynch to Margaret Wilson, Recently converted. Chas. B. Maguire, Pastor.

1818.

Berry-Thomas: January 22, 1818, James Berry to Anna Thomas. Witnesses, Frank Kilday and Daniel Harkins. Chas. B. Maguire, Pastor.

Dogherty-Campbell: .... 1818, John Dogherty to Isabella Campbell. Witnesses, Laughlin and Bernard Dougherty. Chas. B. Maguire, Pastor.

Flower-Bricker: .... 1818, on account of the marriage ceremony having been performed before a Lutheran Minister, it was again performed according to the Rites of the Roman Catholic Church between Valentine Flower of the Catholic Religion and Margaret Bricker a Lutheran. Witnesses, Michael and John Maguire. Charles B. Maguire, Pastor.

Original book, page 130.

Miller-Keiger: ...... 1818, Peter Miller a Catholic to Elizabeth Keiger a non-Catholic. Witnesses, John Miller, the father and a brother of the bridegroom. Chas. B. Maguire, Pastor.

Campbell-Drun: September 16, 1818, Cornelius Campbell to Susan Drun. Witnesses, Joseph Smith and William Bodenhammer.

Aron-Seifert. November 24, 1818, Daniel Aron to Mary Seifert. Witnesses, Thomas Aron and Daniel Kreth. C. B. Maguire, Pastor.

Molloney-O'Dogharty: December 17, 1818, John Molloney to Johanna O'Dogharty. Witnesses, Bernard and John O'Dogharty, brothers of the bride.

Campbell-Cowan: December 20, 1818, John Campbell to Isabella Cowan. Witnesses, Edward Toner and Cornelius Campbell.

Easley-Lingel: November 14, 1818, Gasper Easley to Rachel Lingel. Witnesses, Conrad Henry and Adam Coon.

Original book, page 131.

Short-Karrigan: December 19, 1818, Samuel Short to Mary Karrigan. Witnesses, Michael Maguire and William Dolzin.

Miller-Maguire: .... 1818, James Miller to Mary Maguire. Witnesses, George Miller and Peter Eckroth.

Maguire-Miller: On the same day (date not given however) Prendergast Maguire to Sarah Miller. Witnesses, George Miller and Peter Eckroth.

Buck-Eckroth: February 1, (probably 1819) Joseph Buck to Elizabeth Eckroth. Witnesses, Edward Toner, and Bernard McManus.

Klinger-Sneider, February 10, (probably 1819) John Klinger to Christina Sneider. Witnesses, Joseph and Daniel Aron.

McChristol-Martin: May 24, (probably 1819) Patrick McChristol to Mary Martin. Witnesses, John Martin and Patrick O'Neill.

Maguire-Maguire: May 25, (probably 1819) Patrick Maguire to Susan Maguire. Witnesses, Michael Maguire and Edward Toner.

Original book, page 133.

McMullen-McFie: November 6, A. D. 1821, John McMullen to Mary McFie. Witnesses, Daniel Barr and James Heeny. Rev. Ter. McGirr.

Rensel-Rensell: On the same day by the same, Anthony Rensel to Elizabeth Rensell. Witnesses, Joseph Hanlin and Mardokeus Reed.

O'Brien-Dougherty: February 12, A. D. 1822, by the same, Thomas O'Brien to Elizabeth Dougherty (widow). Witnesses, Patrick McDermott and Bernard McManus.

Aron-Ruffener: July 12, 1822, by the same, George Aron to Margaret Ruffener. Witnesses, Jacob Coon and Joseph Aron.

McClean-Leadin: July 16, 1822, by the same, George McClean non-Catholic to Mary Leadin Catholic. Witnesses, James Toner and James Leadin.

[Note. One entry cut out.]

Sweeny-Ferry: August 12, 1822, by the same, Patrick Sweeny to Anna Ferry. Witnesses, Jacob Khuns and Joseph Henry Khuns.

Hearkins-McKiver: September ...., 1822, by the same, John Hearkins to Eleanor McKiver. Witnesses, Charles Duffy, Mary Hearkins and Bridget McCrea.

Toner-Leadin: October 10, 1822, by the same, Meredith Toner to Anna Leadin. Witnesses, Peter Toner and John Leadin.

Original book, page 134.

Kelly-Toner: November 10, 1822, by the same, Michael Kelly to Anna Toner. Witnesses, Philip McBride and John Toner.

Brown-McGuire: November 11, 1822, by the same, John Brown to Eleanor McGuire. Witnesses, James Brown and James Carthy.

Skelly-Eastly: December 6, by the same, Hugo Skelly to Mary Eastly. Witnesses, Dionysius Connor and Edward Toner.

Heeny-McFie: December 26, 1822, by the same, James Heeny to Margaret McFie. Witnesses, John Toner and William McFie.

Boner-Curran: February 3, A. D. 1823, by the same, Dionysius Boner to Catherine Curran. Witnesses, Bernard McGirr and John Boyle.

Sindoff-Fry: Date not given, Jacob Sindoff to Margaret Fry. Witnesses, John Sindoff and John Henry.

McBride-Sindoff: On the same day (date not given, however) James McBride to Margaret Sindoff. Witnesses, Henry Sindoff, John Henry, Mrs. Khuns.

[Note: These two ceremonies were evidently performed by Father McGirr, although the words "the same" were omitted from the records. L. F. F.]

McKenna-Toner: February 10, 1823, by the same, Patrick McKenna to Margaret Toner. Witnesses Edward Toner, Wilson Jack, Peter Toner and Edward Muldoon.

Kelly-Eastly: June 22, 1824, by the same, Patrick Kelly to Margaret Eastly. Witnesses, Laughlin, Dougherty, and Michael McKenna.

Orignal book, page 135.

Flower-Crete: August 1, 1824, by the same, Valentine Flower to Mary Crete. Witnesses, Edward Toner and Daniel Crete.

Daughan-Duers: November 2, 1824, by the same, John Daughan to Cecilia Duers. Witnesses, Patrick Summers and Thos. Donnelly.

Markle-Kintz: January 9, 1826, by the same, John Markle to Elizabeth Kintz. Witnesses, Jacob Kintz and Joseph Henry.

Kintz-Hanlin: January 9, by the same, George Kintz to Mary Hanlin. Witnesses, Jacob Kintz and Arthur Toner.

Turner-Mullen: June 10, 1826. Bernard Turner to Rachael Mullen. Witnesses James Kenny, James Cain and Charles Finly.

Flower-Bridge: July 1, 1826, by the same, John Flower to Mary Bridge. Witnesses, Michael Crete and George Bridge.

Sindoff-Watterson: November 20, 1826, by the same, Henry Sindoff to Mary Ann Watterson. Witnesses, John Henry and John Watterson.

[Space for 4 entries.]

Original book, page 136.

McBride-McDermott. February A. D. 1827, by the same, Philip McBride to Mary McDermott. Witnesses, Bernard and Eleanor McGirr.

Smith-Crete: May 1, 1827, by the same, Joseph Smith to Sarah Crete. Witnesses, Philip and Daniel Crete.

[½ page space.]

Original book, page 137.

Donnelly-O'Donell: May 30, 1827, by the same, Michael Donnelly to Sarah O'Donell. Witness, Cornelius Rodgers and Madame Montgomery. Rev. Ter. McGirr.

McBride-McBride: July 26, 1827, James McBride to Catherine McBride. Witnesses, Bernard McGinly and ...... (name not given nor "by the same" entered on the record.)

Eastly-Adams: May 3, A. D. 1828, James Eastly to Martha Adams. Witnesses, Jaspar Eastly and his wife. Rev. Ter. McGirr.

Galagher-Duff: August 8, 1828, by the same, John Gallagher to Anna Duff. Witnesses, Con. Johnson and Hanna McKever.

Hanlin-Campbell: August 10, 1828, by the same, Walter Hanlin to Sarah Campbell. Witnesses, Philip Campbell and Mary Brauly.

[October ½ page space.]

Original book, page 138.

Hanlin-Burtell: January 22, 1829, Joseph Hanlin to Mary Burtell. Witnesses, James McBride and John Kealer. Rev. Ter. McGirr.

Waterson-Kintz: April 29, 1829, by the same, James Waterson to Mary Kintz. Witnesses, Frederick Kintz and John Waterson.

Lacy-McCrea. November 1, 1829, by the same, James Lacy to Unity McCrea. Witnesses, Bernard McGirr and Mordecai Reed.

Cary-White: November 1, 1829, by the same, Thomas Cary to Mary White. Witnesses, Bernard McGirr and James White.

Meehan-Kelly: February 4, 1830, by the same, Patrick Meehan to Mary Kelly. Witnesses, Bernard McGirr and James McBride.

Cochran-Gililin: March 21, 1830, by the same, Luke Cochran to Anna Gililin. Witnesses, Patrick Kiely, Eugene Gauly and Michael Goldin.

Murphy-Winn: March 23, 1830, by the same, James Murphy to Mary Winn. Witnesses, Bernard McGirr and Patrick Summers.

McEntire-Ryan: April 30, 1830, Eugene McEntire to Eleanor Ryan. Witnesses, Lawrence Mansfield and Eleanor McGirr.

O'Neil-McCrea: May 10, 1830, by the same, Daniel O'Neil to Bridget McCrea. Witnesses, Cornelius Harkins and Lady Heany.

RECORD OF FUNERALS.

1800.

Original book, page 81.

Under the administration of Rev. Peter Helbron.

Maloscoy, John, April 4, having died suddenly was buried outside the cemetery.

1803.

Barbara, Mary, aged 97, died on September 8, 1803, and was buried in the cemetery.

1804.

———, Margaret, aged 23 years, died on March 1, buried in the cemetery.

Brick, Mary Elizabeth, died June 16, 2 months old. Daughter of Henry Brick.

1808.

Kuhn, Henry, died June 24.

1809.

Moholland, James, 6 years ald, son of David Moholland, buried the 30th.

1810.

Grünewald, Catherine, widow, died ...... (date not given.)

1814.

Brick, Matthias, having been provided with all the Sacraments, died (date not given).

Original book, page 148.

The heading "Record of Funerals" under the administration of Father Charles Bonaventure Maguire of Ireland of the order of the Minor Friars of the Strict Observation, in the capacity of pastor in the year of our Lord

1818.

Colter, James, died January 21, having been born 2 weeks before, was buried in the cemetery.

Brück, George, died in the 22nd year of his age on January 25, was buried in the cemetery.

Sheridan, William, son of John, died on February 5, having been born 3 months before, was buried in the cemetery.

Henry, James, in his 31st year (died on March 8th), having received all the Sacraments, was buried in the cemetery.

Brück, Margaret, in her 27th year, died February 6, buried in the cemetery.

Hayney, John, died February 9, in his 52nd year, was buried in the cemetery.

Mergel, Catherine, 3 months old, died June 5th, buried in the cemetery.

Original book, page 147.

1819.

Rufner, Catherine, wife of Mr. Simon Rufner in her .... year, died February 12, was buried in the cemetery.

Flour, John, in his 49th year, died April 20, was buried in the cemetery.

Flour, Daniel, son of John and Anna Mary Flour in his 2nd year, died April 21st, and was buried in the cemetery.

Rogers, Peter, aged ...., died June 12th and was buried in the cemetery.

Miller, Anna, in her 71st year, died June 18th and was buried in the cemetery.

Brogan, Sarah, daughter of Charles and Agnes Brogan, 3 years old, died July 13th, and was buried in the cemetery.

Huntsberger, Anna Mary Catherine, died of a snake bite at the age of 38. July 14th, and was buried in the cemetery.

Donnelly, Simon, died July 21, at the age of 28 and was buried in the cemetery.

Thomas, Margaret, died on August 29th at the age of 59 and was buried in the cemetery.

O'Connor, James, and ...... children of John and Sarah O'Connor, that one ...... died on the same day.

Original book, page 146.

O'Connor, Anna, died on August 30, ..., ... years old, and was buried in the cemetery.

Harkins, Bridget, daughter of Daniel and Margaret Harkins, 3 days old, died in December, (date not given) and was buried in the cemetery.

Original book, page 154.

Paschal Confessions were heard by Rev. Peter Helbron, Pastor, for the year, in the years and in the number of penitents as below.

1801	Confessions,	74	1809	Confessions,	174
1802	″	105	1810	″	120
1803	″	126	1811	″	173
1804	″	128	1812	″	162
1805	″	132	1813	″	170
1806	″	134	1814	″	171
1807	″	145	1815	″	165
1808	″	168			

Carr (cont.)
Charles 17, 39
Crescentia 50
Frances 60
Helen 35
James 17, 35
Manasses 17, 35, 50,
60
Margaret 17
Mary (Mrs.) 35
Patrick 17, 35, 60
Petronilla (Mrs.) 35,
60
Susan 17
Susan (Mrs.) 17
Theresa 35
see Car
Carren, John 48
Margaret (Mrs.) 48
Salome 48
Carrien, Peter 66
Prudentia (Mrs.) 66
Carriens (Cairns), Mary
35
Carriens (Kerens?), Mary
35
Carrigan, Peter 64
Prudentia (Mrs.) 64
Carroll, (?) (Bis.) 8
John (Rev.) 12
see Carl
see Carole
Carry, Margaret (Mrs.)
27
Michael 27
Carry (Carey?), Joseph
27
Carter, see Carder
Carthy, James 96
Cary, Catharine 53
Susan (Mrs.) 53, 62
Thomas 98
Timothy 53, 62
Cary (Carey?), Rose 62
Cassidy, Anna 90
Bridget 86
Bridget (Mrs.) 86, 90
Patrick 86, 90
Caster, Mary 50
Casthler, Mary 48
Cembor, Barbara (Mrs.)
44
John 44
Cembor (Kemper?),
Anthony 44
Chalegar (Gallagher?),
John 48
Champbell (Campbell?),
Andrew 24
Catharine (Mrs.) 24
Margaret (Mrs.) 24
Michael 24
Chartery, Daniel 32
Helen 32
Helen (Mrs.) 32
Chevlin, Edward 76, 83
Christy, Archibald 30
Mary (Mrs.) 30
Peter 30
Cifiny, Salome 52
Cinckley, Mary 43
Cinnen, Jeremiah 38
Margaret (Mrs.) 38
Cinnen (Keenan?),
Elizabeth 38
Margaret 38
Mary Anne 38
William 38

Cipphers, Elizabeth 86
Clany, Mary 31
Claudwill, (?) (Mrs.) 46
Andrew 46
Clearfield, Peter 35
Clearsen, (?) 47
Clenegal, Helen 45
Hughy 45
Mary (Mrs.) 45
Clerick, Catharine 20
Catharine (Mrs.) 34
Daniel 20, 33
Elizabeth 34
Helen (Mrs.) 37
Helena (Mrs.) 33
Jacob 34
John 37
Mary (Mrs.) 20
Rose 37
Sara (Mrs.) 20
Clerin, Elizabeth 23
Helen (Mrs.) 23
John 23
Clinger, Catharine 32,
72
Clugency, John 40
Margaret 40
Mary (Mrs.) 40
Cochran, Luke 98
Cohl (Cole?), Margaret
19
Cohl (Kohl?), Margaret
19
Cole, see Cohl
Coleman, see Collman
Coll, Anna 17, 18, 60
Crescentia 54
Eppy 48
James 54, 60
Maggy 85
Margaret 56
Mary 69
Matilda 84
Salome (Mrs.) 54, 60
Collen, Catharine (Mrs.)
55
Patrick 55
William 55
Collen (Collins?), Mary
21
Collenz, Julia (Mrs.) 30
William 30
Collenz (Collins?),
Charles 30
John 30
William 30
Coller, Catharine (Mrs.)
22
George 22
John 22
Magdalen (Mrs.) 40
Mary 22, 40
Michael 40
Collerick, Ann (Mrs.)
22, 23
Charles 53
Henry 22
John 22, 23
Mary 22
Collerik, Anna 52
Collfy, Margaret 59
Collins, see Callenz
see Collen
see Collenz
Collman, John 32
Mary (Mrs.) 32
Collman (Coleman?), Anna
32

Colter, James 99
Commery, Daniel 38
Margaret (Mrs.) 38
Conley, see Konnly
Connelly, John 78, 80
Conner, Anna 69
Catharine 16
Daniel 16
Dennis 75
Dionysius 21, 33, 46,
58, 60, 63, 66, 83,
93
Elizabeth 15, 46
Graffert 21
Helen 66
Helen (Mrs.) 70
James 60
John 57, 58, 66
Magdalen (Mrs.) 16,
63, 66
Margaret 33, 53, 93
Mary 16
Mary (Mrs.) 58, 60, 75
Petronilla 63, 69
Petronilla (Mrs.) 51,
57, 58
Salome 16, 63
Susan (Mrs.) 21
Thadeus 15
Thomas 16
Timothy 35, 51, 53,
58, 69, 70
William 21, 66
Connery, Anna 71
Maurice 71
Sarah (Mrs.) 71
Connor, Dionysius 96
Margaret 21
Mary 92
Timothy 21
Conor, (?) (Mrs.) 86
Dionysius 86
John 86
Margaret Lusilda 86
Mary 86
Mary (Mrs.) 86
Sarah (Mrs.) 86
Conway, Hugh 86
Coogen, Elfy 59
Coon, Adam 74, 81, 91,
95
Catharine (Mrs.) 80,
86, 88
Cornelius 91
Daniel 79
Elizabeth 75
Elizabeth (Mrs.) 76,
83, 88, 90
George 73, 75, 77, 83,
87, 89, 90, 91
Henry 80, 86, 88
Jacob 73, 74, 75, 79,
83, 85, 87, 89, 96
Leo 90
Mary 73
Mary (Mrs.) 73, 74,
75, 79, 83, 87, 89,
90, 91
Mary Ann 74
Mary Magdalen 91
Mary Sibylla 76
Rachel 84
Rachel (Mrs.) 74, 91
Regina (Mrs.) 81
Solomon 76, 83, 88, 90
Susan 89
Susan Catherine 88
William Jacob 90

Coon (Kuhn?), Catharine
  Anna 79
  Jacob 83
  Mary 77
  Rose 81
Coon (Kuhn??), Mary
  Matilda 83
Cornin, Charles 83
  Margaret 83
  Susan (Mrs.) 83
Corr, Margaret (Mrs.) 71
  Peter 71
Corrh--, Ann 50
Corrigen, Michael 61
  Peter 61
  Prudy (Mrs.) 61
Corry (Curry?), Margaret
  21
Cowan, Isabella 95
Coyl, Catharine (Mrs.)
  77
  Mary 77
  Philip 77
Coyle, see Koyl
Craig, see Crecck
  see Creck
Crait, Catharine 73
  Daniel 73
  Sara (Mrs.) 73
Crate, Michael 75
Cread, Theresa 67, 70
Crecck, Ann (Mrs.) 34
  Joseph 34
Crecck (Craig?),
  Prudentia 34
Creck, Anna (Mrs.) 34
  Joseph 34
Creck (Craig?), Nicholas
  34
Cred, Daniel 68, 69
  Johanna 68
  Salome (Mrs.) 68, 69
  Theresa 67, 68
Creeck, Ann (Mrs.) 34
  Joseph 34
Creny, Edward 20
  Elizabeth (Mrs.) 20
  John 20
Crete, Andrew 91
  Daniel 82, 84, 86, 97
  Elizabeth 86
  Elizabeth (Mrs.) 82,
    86
  John 86
  Mary 97
  Michael 84, 86, 97
  Philip 82, 86, 97
  Sarah 97
  Sarah (Mrs.) 82, 84,
    86
  Theresa 82
Croffey, John 18
  Margaret (Mrs.) 18
  Mary 18
Crotty, Anna (Mrs.) 73
  Catharine 73
  Patrick 73
Cull, Annabel 18
  Margery 73
Curran, Catherine 97
  John 71
  Michael 72
Curren, John 64
  Margaret (Mrs.) 64
Curring, John 33
  Margaret (Mrs.) 33
Curring (Curry?), Mary
  33

Curry, Anna (Mrs.) 52
  Bridget 15
  Catharine 19
  Daniel 56
  John 15, 19, 56
  Margaret 91
  Margaret (Mrs.) 56
  William 52
  see Corry
  see Curring
Cypher, Barbara 71
  Elizabeth 73
  Philip 71
Daboy, Lawrence 93
Dagarthy, Ann (Mrs.) 23
  Catharine (Mrs.) 20
  Daniel 23
  James 20
Dagarthy (Dougherty?),
  James 20
  Thomas 23
Dagaurthy, John 51
  Mary (Mrs.) 51
Dagcarthy, Lochly 54
  Salome (Mrs.) 54
Dagcarthy (Dougherty?),
  Eleazer 54
Dagerthy, Anna (Mrs.) 41
  Anne (Mrs.) 23
  Crescentia (Mrs.) 40
  James 23, 41
  Margaret (Mrs.) 21
  Mary 40
  Neal 40
  William 21
Dagerthy (Dougherty?),
  Hughy 41
  James 23
  Patrick 40
Dagerthy (Doughtery?),
  William 21
Dagethy, Anna (Mrs.) 18
  James 18
Dagethy (Dougherty?),
  James 18
  Patrick 18
Dageurthy, Catharine
  (Mrs.) 25
  James 25
  John 25
  Margaret (Mrs.) 25
  Susan (Mrs.) 25
  William 25
Dageurthy (Dougherty?),
  James 25
  John 25
  Sara 25
Dagharty, Lachelin 57
  Sallie (Mrs.) 57
Dagharty (Dougherty?),
  Thomas 57
Dagourthy, Ann (Mrs.) 27
  Anna 36
  Anna (Mrs.) 32, 36
  Catharine 38
  Catharine (Mrs.) 34
  Charles 36
  Crescentia (Mrs.) 50
  Daniel 34
  Eleanor (Mrs.) 37
  Elizabeth 37
  Elizabeth (Mrs.) 33
  Isabella (Mrs.) 49
  James 32, 33, 49
  John 32
  Manasses 34
  Margaret (Mrs.) 58,
    64, 68

Dagourthy (cont.)
  Nicholas 50
  Patrick 27
  Petronilla 50
  Roger 37
  Susan (Mrs.) 32
  William 58, 64, 68
Dagourthy (Dougherty?),
  Bridget (Mrs.) 49
  Catharine (Mrs.) 29
  Edward 30
  John Benjamin 49
  John 26
  Mary 25, 37
  Michael 49
  Margaret 33
  Patrick 32
  Peter 29
  Sara 27
Dagouthy (Dougherty?),
  Bridget 34
Daguorthy, Anna (Mrs.)
  36
  Charles 36
Daguorthy (Dougherty?),
  (?) 36
Daiman, Eleanor (Mrs.)
  44
  Jacob 43
  John 43, 44
  Petronilla (Mrs.) 44
  William 43
Daiman (Diamond?),
  Daniel 44
  Joseph 43
  Petronilla 44
  Philip 44
Daniel, Charity (Mrs.)
  37
  Felix 37
  Mary 37
Dannely (Donnelly?),
  Patrick 52
Dannly, Charity (Mrs.)
  20
  Felix 20
Dannly (Donnelly?),
  Charity 20
  Isabel 20
Dapper, Catharine 63
  Catherine 94
  Elizabeth 93
  Margaret 94
Darby, (?) 36
  Catharine (Mrs.) 21
  Mary (Mrs.) 36
  Nicholas 21
Dauff, (?) 51
  Johanna (Mrs.) 51
  Paul 51
Dauffy, Patrick 54
Dauffy (Duffy?),
  Margaret Corry
  (Mrs.) 51
  Philip 51
Daugerthy, Anna (Mrs.)
  47
  Bridget 47
  James 47
  John 33
  Margaret (Mrs.) 33
  William 33
Daugerthy (Dougherty),
  Bernard 14
Daugethy (Dougherty?),
  Catharine 21
Daughan, John 97

105

108

Mecbraid (McBride?)
(cont.) Margaret 53
Mary 40
Mary (Mrs.) 42, 43, 45
Neal 43, 45 '
Patrick 42, 43, 45
Petronilla 48
Stephen 42
Mecbraidt, Barbara
(Mrs.) 62
James 62
Mecbraigd, Nicholas 63
Sibylla (Mrs.) 63
Mecbraigd (McBride?),
Nicholas 63
Mecbraigdt, Nicholas 63
MeccShery, Angus 26
Isabel (Mrs.) 26
Meccaffry, Hugo 52
Margaret (Mrs.) 52
Meccanhenny (McAnany?),
Henry 15
Meccanigen, (?) (Mrs.)
37
Julius 37
Petronilla (Mrs.) 37
Meccannell, Jacob 53
Mary (Mrs.) 53
Meccannell (McConnell?),
Genevieve 53
Meccbraid, (?) (Mrs.) 39
Mary (Mrs.) 50
Nicholas 39
Thomas 50
Meccbraid (McBride?),
George Car 50
Margaret 39
Neal 35
Meccdamerd (McDermott?),
Bridget 50
Meccdamert (McDermott?),
Patrick 50
Meccedell, Elizabeth 49
Elizabeth (Mrs.) 49
Patrick 49
Meccefferty, Catharine
(Mrs.) 48
Jacob 48
Meccefferty
(McCafferty?),
Charles 48
Meccelray, Charles 63
Mary (Mrs.) 63
Meccelray (McElroy?),
Mary 63
Meccenaldy, Peter 57
Meccfaull, John 52
Mary (Mrs.) 52
Meccfaull (McFaul?),
James 52
Meccfergin, Catharine
(Mrs.) 23
Charles 23
Edward 23
Helen (Mrs.) 23
Meccferling, Catharine
(Mrs.) 23
Edward 23
Meccferling (McFarlane),
Edward 23
Meccferly, Catharine
(Mrs.) 39
Charles 39
Manasses 39
Margaret 22
Margaret (Widow) 92
Meccferren, Edward 36
Eva (Mrs.) 36

Meccferrien, Anna (Mrs.)
54
Catharine 54
Catharine (Mrs.) 54
John 54
Meccferring, John 50
Meccferrling, Bridget
(Mrs.) 50
Catharine 50
Charles 50
Edward 50
Meccferry, Anna (Mrs.)
34
Catharine (Mrs.) 34
Edward 34
Joseph 34
Neal 34
Meccfolh (McFaul?),
Genevieve (Mrs.) 37
James 37
Rose 37
Meccfoull (McFaul?), Ann
45
John 45
Meccful, James 49
Meccfull (McFaul?),
Helen 49
Meccginley, Catharine
(Mrs.) 54
James 54
Meccginley (McKinley?),
James 54
Meccginly, Catharine
(Mrs.) 54
James 54
Meccginly (McKinley?),
James 54
Meccginly (McKinly?),
John 53
Meccguy, Michael 39
Petronilla (Mrs.) 39
Meccguy (McHugh?),
Catharine 39
Margaret 39
Meccgynly, Bridget
(Mrs.) 93
James 93
Meccherry, Catharine
(Mrs.) 48
Gerhard 48
Meccherry (McSherry?),
Gerard 47
Margaret 48
Mecchery (McSherry?),
(?) 38
Mecchiffisen, Bridget
(Mrs.) 37
Patrick 37
Meccingly, Bridget
(Mrs.) 50
Edward 50
John 50
Mary (Mrs.) 50
Meccingly (McKinley),
Edward 50
Meccingly (McKinley,
Catharine (Mrs.) 50
Meccingly (McKinley?),
James 50
Mecciven (McIvan?),
Elizabeth 65
Meccshery, Angus 26
Bartholomew 26
Isabel (Mrs.) 26
Meccshery (McSherry?),
Bartholomew 26
Meccu, Charles 16
Meccu (McHugh?), Anna

Meccu (McHugh?), Anna
Catharine 16
Macdarmet, Bridget
(Mrs.) 57
Mecdarmet, Patrick 57
Mecdarmet (McDermott?),
William 57
Mecdarmor, Bridget
(Mrs.) 59
Mary 59
Patrick 59
Mecdavid, Patrick 93
Mecdemard, Bridget
(Mrs.) 63
Patrick 63
Salome 63
Mecdemart (McDermott?),
Bridget 47
Mecdonnel, (?) 46
Rose (Mrs.) 46
Mecdonnel (McDonald?),
Rose 46
Mecdonnell, Anna 65
Anna (Mrs.) 57
Cecilia (Mrs.) 65
Cornelius 57
Dionysius 65
James 57
Patrick 57
Meceelfrey, Patrick 53
Sophie (Mrs.) 53
Mecenaldy, (?) 56
Anna Maria 56
Catharine (Mrs.) 56
Sara 56
Mecfaull, John 55
Martha (Mrs.) 55
Mecfee, Anna (Mrs.) 60,
62
Elizabeth 62
Patrick 60, 62
Salome 60
Mecferien, Charles 35
Genevieve (Mrs.) 35
Mecferry, Daniel 35
Susan (Mrs.) 35
Timothy 35
Mecferryn, Sophie 48
Mecfferrien, Edward 44
Mecfoll (McFaul?), James
36
Mecgill, Bridget (Mrs.)
71
James 71
Joseph 71
Mecgirley, Bridget
(Mrs.) 54
Edward 54
Mecgiven, John 50
Mary (Mrs.) 50
Nicholas 50
Mecgready, John 71
Mary (Mrs.) 71
Patrick 71
Mechachen, Andrew 54
Arthur 54
Elizabeth 55
James 54
Joseph 54
Margaret (Mrs.) 54
Mary 55
Sara 54
Mechafly, (?) 36
Anna 36
Eleanor (Mrs.) 36
Mecherrikell, Anna
(Mrs.) 29
James 29

Mecherrikell
(McGarrigle?), Anna
29
Mechin, John 14
Mechin (Maginn?), James
14
Mechin (McKean?), James
14
Mechyn, Berny 35
Salome (Mrs.) 35
Mechyn (Maginn), Joseph
35
Mechyn (McKean?), Joseph
35
Meciver (McIvor?),
Michael 67
Mecivestin, Anna (Mrs.)
52
James 52
Meckbraid, Bridget
(Mrs.) 27
John 29
Mary (Mrs.) 29
Neal 92
Patrick 27
Meckbraid (McBride?),
Bridget 27
Margaret 29
Meckderrly, Anna 27
Cornelius 27
Mary (Mrs.) 27
Meckeen, James 50
Meckeen (McKean?), Mary
50
Meckeley, Daniel 41
John 41
Susan (Mrs.) 41
Meckelfee, Anna (Mrs.)
68
Daniel 68
Patrick 68
Meckelfy, Anna (Mrs.) 54
James 54
Patrick 54
Meckellfy (McKelvey?),
Patrick 30
Meckellrey (McElroy?),
Mary (Mrs.) 41
Patrick 41
Meckelly, (?) 45
Bridget 27
Catharine (Mrs.) 27
William 27
Meckelrey (McElroy?),
Philip 29
Meckelwe, Anna (Mrs.) 18
Patrick 18
Meckelwe (McKelvey?),
Mary 18
Meckenalldy, James 44
Mary (Mrs.) 44
Meckenalldy (McNulty?),
James 44
Meckenelly (McAnally?),
George 28
Meckenenny (McAnany),
Henry 18
Meckenhady, Mary 44
Meckennegy, Anna 37
Meckenolly, Catharine 28
Mary (Mrs.) 27
Patrick 27
Meckenolly (McAnally?),
Julius 27
Meckeny, (?) 43
Margaret (Mrs.) 43
Meckeny (McKenna?),
Bartholomew 43

Meckerr, John 25
Petronilla (Mrs.) 25
Meckerr (McGirr?),
William 25
Meckever, Anna (Mrs.) 18
Patrick 18
Meckever (McKeever?),
Anna 18
Meckfall (McFaul?),
Catharine 25
James 24
John 25
Meckferling (McFarlane),
Daniel 18
Meckferring, Charles 29
Edward 29
Mary (Mrs.) 29
Meckferrly, Anna (Mrs.)
29
Edward 28, 29
Margaret (Mrs.) 28
Meckferry, Cornelius 27
Mary (Mrs.) 27
Meckfuy, Anna (Mrs.) 31
Patrick 31
Meckfuy (McVey?),
Margaret 31
Meckfy, Anna (Mrs.) 19
Anne (Mrs.) 18
Patrick 18, 19
Meckfy (McVey?), John 18
Mary 19
Michael 18
Meckiffisin, Anna 38
Meckingly (McKinley?),
Catharine (Mrs.) 39
James 39
Meckiver, John 48
Mary (Mrs.) 48
Mecknenning (McAnany),
Joanna 17
Meckohl, James 29
Petronilla (Mrs.) 29
Meckohl (McCall?),
Elizabeth 29
Meckuy, Bridget (Mrs.)
29
Daniel 29
Joseph 28
Margaret 92
Mary (Mrs.) 28
Meckuy (McHugh?),
Bridget (Mrs.) 29
Bridget 29
Daniel 29
Elizabeth 26
Isabel 19
James 29
Margaret 18
Michael 26
Rose 28
Meckyu, Sibbila 92
Meclachelen, Anna (Mrs.)
45, 62
Henry 45
Patrick 62
William 45
Meclachelen
(McLaughlin?),
Bernard 62
Thomas 45
Meclachlen, (?) (Mrs.)
45
Anne (Mrs.) 28
Henry 45
John 45
Patrick 28

Meclachlen (McLaughlin?)
(cont.) John
30
(?) (Mrs.) 38
Anna (Mrs.) 30
Meclachlen (McLaughlin),
Thomas 38
Meclachlen
(McLaughlin?), James
28, 41
Meclagden, Anna 66
Mary 66
Michael 66
Rose (Mrs.) 66
William 66
Meclaglen, John 70
Meclaglen (McLaughlin?),
James 66
Meclansy, Morrall 28
Neal 56
Nicholas 26
Treys (Mrs.) 28
Meclansy (McGlinchy?),
Neal 18
Meclany (McIlhenny?),
John 25
Meclarsy, Neal 36
Meclay, Catharine (Mrs.)
29
John 29
William 29
Meclean, John 69
Margaret 69
Rose (Mrs.) 69
Mecloden, Mary 20
Mecloscy (McCloskey?),
James 40
Meclosscy, (?) (Mrs.) 40
John 39, 40
Nicholas 40
Rose (Mrs.) 39
Meclosscy (McCloskey?),
Daniel 39
John 39
James 40
Michael 40
Petronilla 39
Meclvay (McKelvey?), (?)
40
Margaret (Mrs.) 40
Mecmolland, Catharine
(Mrs.) 57
Inos 57
Margaret 57
Mecneckel, Gabriel 43
Margaret (Mrs.) 43
Meconly, John 70
Mary (Mrs.) 70
Mecquier (McGuire?),
Patrick 47
Mecquire (McGuire?),
James 53
Petronilla (Mrs.) 53
Mecschiveston, Patrick
55
Meehan, James 87
Patrick 98
Roger H. 87
see Mehann
see Michen
see Migen
Meehen, see Michen
Meganey, James 23
Megardy, Elizabeth
(Mrs.) 51
Patrick 51
Megardy (McCarthy?),
Elizabeth 51

118

121